WHITE HOUSE SECRETS

MEDICAL LIES AND COVER-UPS

WHITE HOUSE SECRETS

MEDICAL LIES AND COVER-UPS

GAIL JARROW

CALKINS CREEK
AN IMPRINT OF ASTRA BOOKS FOR YOUNG READERS
NEW YORK

For information about permission to reproduce selections from this book, please
contact permissions@astrapublishinghouse.com.

Calkins Creek
An imprint of Astra Books for Young Readers, a division of Astra Publishing House
astrapublishinghouse.com
Printed in Malaysia

ISBN: 978-1-6626-8103-5 (hc)
ISBN: 978-1-6626-8104-2 (eBook)
The Library of Congress Cataloging-in-Publication Data is available upon request.

First edition
10 9 8 7 6 5 4 3 2 1

Design by Red Herring Design
The text is set in Chaparral.
The titles are set in Veneer.

CONTENTS

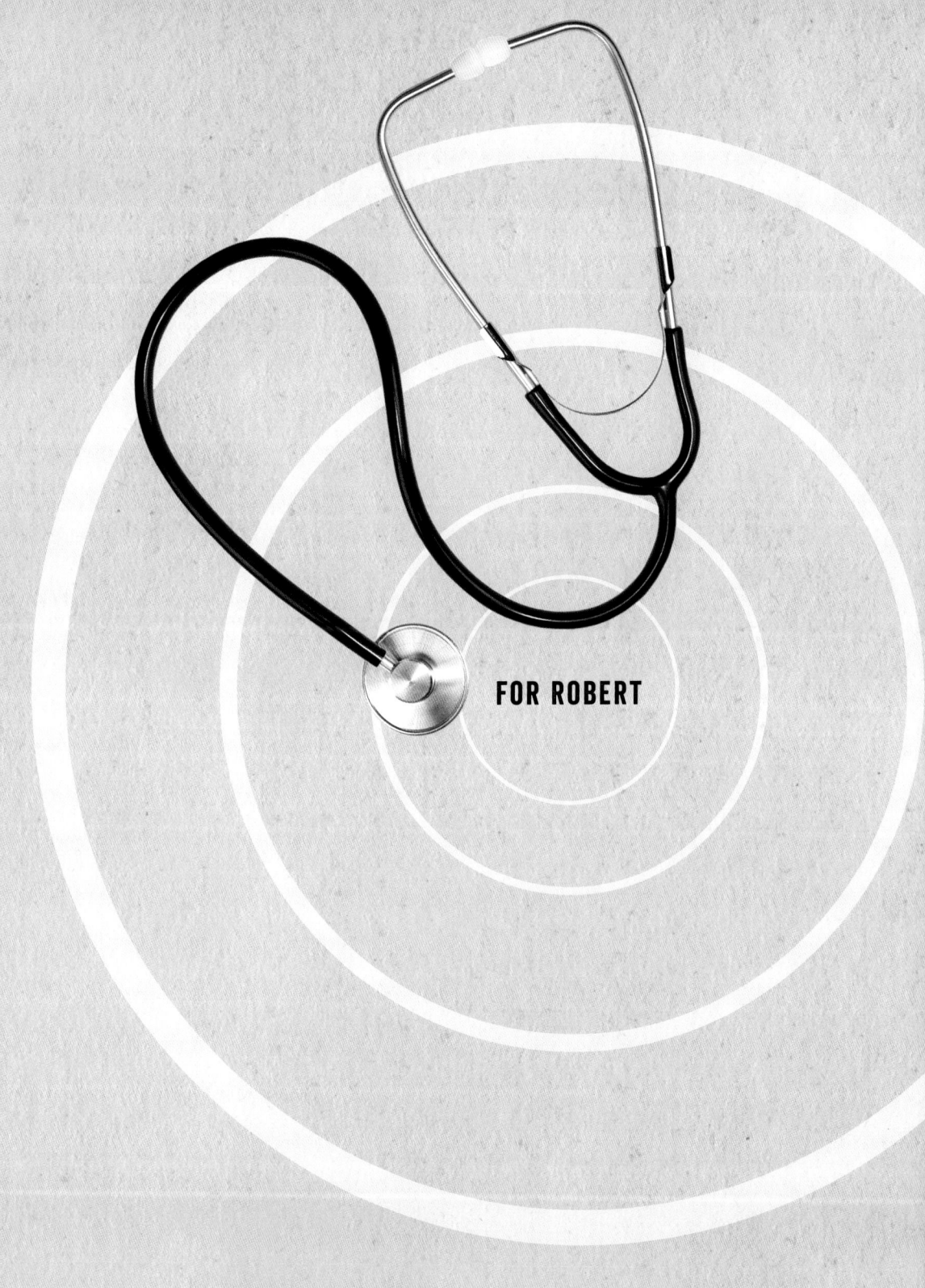

FOR ROBERT

WELCOME TO THE WHITE HOUSE

EIGHT UNITED STATES PRESIDENTS DIED IN OFFICE. MORE THAN A THIRD of the chief executives became seriously ill during their terms. Yet at times, Americans were deliberately kept in the dark about the health crisis in the White House. Lies were told. Cover-ups were orchestrated.

Some of these cases were medical fiascoes. A slow, painful death caused by outdated physician practices. A misdiagnosed condition that was incorrectly treated. An incapacitating stroke hidden from the cabinet and the public. A dying president campaigning for another term while the country was at war. The dangerous use of painkillers and pep pills by the world's most powerful leader.

Disasters were narrowly averted. A secret surgery aboard a yacht. A concealed illness that almost set off a leadership crisis. Certain death prevented by a Secret Service agent's quick thinking. A president's attempt to run for reelection when many doubted that he could finish a second term.

In the eighteenth and early nineteenth centuries, the press rarely discussed the health of the president. Communication then was so slow that an ailing president likely recovered before the nation knew he'd been ill.

In those days, it wasn't unusual for people—including presidents—to get sick. Pneumonia and tuberculosis killed millions. Deadly intestinal diseases like cholera, typhoid fever, and dysentery spread when human waste contaminated drinking water. Malaria and yellow fever afflicted those bitten by mosquitoes that bred in swamps and standing water. The dangerous childhood diseases diphtheria, measles, mumps, whooping cough, scarlet fever, and polio snuffed out the lives of the young before they made it to adulthood.

The medical community had little to offer a sick person. Doctor training was brief and superficial. Surgery was risky and often impossible to do without killing the patient. Remedies were typically ineffective. Treatments, such as bleeding, were harmful and weakened the victim. People either died quickly or recovered in spite of the doctor's actions.

A patient's chances didn't improve until the end of the nineteenth century. By then, doctors and scientists understood that germs caused diseases. That breakthrough led to vaccines, including those that protected children from fatal illnesses. Physicians began following antiseptic procedures such as handwashing and using disinfecting chemicals.

Public health measures improved sewage disposal, provided clean drinking water, and drained swamps. Nutrition got better. New antibiotic medicines treated many infections.

In 1900, the leading causes of American deaths were influenza, pneumonia, tuberculosis, and intestinal illnesses. But by 1950, the top killers were heart disease and cancer. This change was reflected in the ailments of the twentieth-century presidents.

As the federal government steadily grew in size and importance after the Civil War, so did the influence of the chief executive. A president's health became a matter of great concern. News traveled faster through newspapers, telegraph, then radio, television, and eventually the internet. The public demanded to know details about the medical condition of its president.

When this interest increased, lies about presidential illnesses did, too. The cover-ups had dramatic consequences for the nation. A few of the deceptions remained hidden for decades.

Here are the shocking true stories of these White House medical secrets.

EIGHT PRESIDENTS DIED IN OFFICE

William Henry Harrison (1841; illness)

Zachary Taylor (1849–1850; illness)

Abraham Lincoln (1861–1865; assassinated)

James Garfield (1881; assassinated)

William McKinley (1897–1901; assassinated)

Warren Harding (1921–1923; illness)

Franklin Roosevelt (1933–1945; illness)

John Kennedy (1961–63; assassinated)

JAMES GARFIELD

BORN: November 19, 1831, in Orange, Ohio

PROFESSION BEFORE PRESIDENCY: teacher, college president, preacher, army general, lawyer, U.S. congressman from Ohio

POLITICAL PARTY: Republican

ELECTED: 1880

SERVED: March 1881 to September 1881

DIED: September 19, 1881, in Elberon, New Jersey, age forty-nine

PRESIDENTIAL TRIVIA:

★ Garfield was the last president born in a log cabin.

★ Garfield was the first president whose mother was present at her son's inauguration.

James Abram Garfield in 1880, the year he was elected president

CHAPTER ONE
DOOMED BY DIRTY FINGERS

"What have I done, that this must come to me."
—JAMES GARFIELD

FROM LOG CABIN TO WHITE HOUSE

JAMES GARFIELD NEEDED A VACATION. DURING THE FIRST FOUR MONTHS of his presidency, he'd found the job to be a headache. In fact, he'd experienced frequent headaches from the endless trail of people wanting jobs in his new administration.

Now at the end of June 1881, Garfield looked forward to his upcoming trip through New England with his wife, Lucretia, and their three oldest children. After that, they would return to their Mentor, Ohio, farm for the rest of the summer where they'd reunite with the two youngest Garfield children.

The vacation would never happen.

James Abram Garfield had come a long way from his birth in an Ohio log cabin. His rise from poverty to the presidency didn't surprise those who knew him. He was intelligent, well educated, ambitious, and amiable. At a time when politicians were often judged by their oratory abilities, Garfield was a skilled debater and rousing speaker.

In June 1880, as the presidential election approached, the Republican Party met in Chicago to choose its nominee. The sitting Republican president, Rutherford Hayes (1877–1881), had announced that he wouldn't run for reelection. A battle broke out within the party.

One faction, nicknamed the Stalwarts, was led by Senator Roscoe Conkling of New York. During Hayes's presidency, the Stalwarts lost the power to influence government appointments that they'd enjoyed under the two terms of Hayes's predecessor, President Ulysses Grant (1869–1877). They supported Grant for a third term. The other faction considered Grant a losing candidate because of the scandals and corruption during his eight years in office. This group supported Senator James Blaine of Maine.

When the convention delegates weren't able to agree on either candidate, they chose James Garfield. He was well known for his seventeen years in Congress and dedication to the Republican Party. He'd shown that he could work with those of different viewpoints. In his stirring address to the delegates, Garfield called for party unity and impressed many in the convention hall.

Republicans knew they needed the backing of Grant, Conkling, and the Stalwarts to rally voters and raise money for the campaign. Without consulting Garfield, his supporters decided to offer the vice presidential nomination to one of Conkling's closest friends, Chester Arthur of New

JAMES A. GARFIELD
REPUBLICAN CANDIDATE FOR PRESIDENT

CHESTER A. ARTHUR
REPUBLICAN CANDIDATE FOR VICE PRESIDENT

York. Arthur had never run for public office, but he was a compromise candidate. Everyone could live with him.

With Arthur on the ticket, Garfield won the presidency on November 2, 1880, beating the Democratic candidate, Winfield Scott Hancock. The election was extremely close. Garfield's margin of victory was only about ten thousand votes, or 0.1 percent of all ballots cast nationwide.

A poster from the 1880 presidential campaign showing the two Republican candidates

VIOLENT ENCOUNTER

On Saturday morning, July 2, 1881, Garfield was finally heading off for his long-anticipated vacation while Congress was out of session. His trusted staff and Secretary of State James Blaine would remain in Washington to handle any problems that might develop.

In fact, one problem had been brewing for months without anyone realizing how serious it had become. A thirty-nine-year-old man named Charles Guiteau had been stalking the president since Garfield's inauguration in early March.

Guiteau had been a failure at most everything he attempted. Born in Illinois in 1841, he tried being a religious commune member, a journalist, an attorney, and a lecturer. The only thing he was good at was manipulating people. Eventually, business associates and friends abandoned him after he swindled them. Family members suspected he was mentally ill.

During the 1880 presidential campaign, Guiteau visited the Republican Party's New York City headquarters. He considered himself friendly with the Stalwarts and Chester Arthur, although the vice presidential candidate barely knew him. Guiteau's role in the election was limited to one speech he gave to a small group. In Guiteau's mind, however, he was key to Garfield's victory. He expected the new president to reward him with an important diplomatic position in the administration.

Early in March 1881, Guiteau headed from New York City to Washington to claim the job. Despite his multiple attempts to see President Garfield and Secretary of State Blaine, the coveted appointment didn't come. Because Guiteau was obviously unqualified and annoyingly persistent, he was banned from the offices of both men. That was when he decided that God was telling him what he had to do: James Abram Garfield had "wrecked the once grand old Republican party, and for this he dies."

Charles Guiteau

After buying a gun, Guiteau followed the president around Washington, waiting for his best shot. Even though President Abraham Lincoln had been assassinated just sixteen years before, Garfield had no bodyguards or police protection when he left the White House.

On July 2, when James Garfield walked through Washington's Baltimore and Potomac Railroad Depot on his way to catch his vacation train, he was accompanied only by James Blaine. As the two men crossed the waiting room engrossed in last-minute conversation before the president's departure, they did not notice Charles Guiteau lurking in the doorway shadows.

Guiteau stepped forward until he was about 6 feet (2 m) from the president. He drew out his gun, aimed at Garfield's back, and pulled the trigger.

Garfield turned toward the sound. "My God! What is this?" he cried. The bullet had struck his upper right arm, causing a minor flesh wound.

Guiteau moved closer and shot again. The president collapsed to the floor.

Charles Guiteau ran but was quickly grabbed by two policemen on duty in the station. As they dragged him outside, he cried, "I did it, and will go to jail for it. Arthur is President, and I am a stalwart."

WOUNDED

Secretary Blaine and several bystanders gathered around the president. Blood covered the floor. Someone sent for the nearest doctor.

Washington's health officer, Dr. Smith Townshend, arrived by Garfield's side within five minutes of the shooting. He found the president still lying on the dirty waiting room floor where he'd fallen.

Townshend asked the president if he was in pain. Garfield replied that he felt a prickling sensation in his right foot and leg. Townshend feared this meant damage to the spine.

FRANK LESLIE'S
ILLUSTRATED
NEWSPAPER

No. 1,346—Vol. LII.   NEW YORK, JULY 16, 1881.   [Price 10 Cents.

WASHINGTON, D. C.—THE ATTACK ON THE PRESIDENT'S LIFE—MRS. SMITH SUPPORTING THE PRESIDENT WHILE AWAITING THE ARRIVAL OF THE AMBULANCE.—From Sketches by our Special Artists A. Berghaus, and C. Upham.—See Page 335.

After Garfield said he could turn onto his side, Townshend lifted up the bloody clothing and checked the president's back. He spotted blood seeping from an entry wound about 4 inches (10 cm) to the right of Garfield's backbone near his waist. Townshend used his finger to remove a small blood clot where the bullet entered. He concluded that the president was mortally wounded.

Soon more doctors arrived to help, including surgeon Dr. D. W. Bliss. Because of his Civil War medical experience, Bliss was considered a gunshot wound expert. He and Garfield had known each other as teens in Ohio.

Bliss immediately took over. Following the U.S. Army's recommended procedure during the war, he checked Garfield's injury by sticking his little finger into the wound. He hoped to feel the bullet near the surface where he could extract it with his instruments. Bliss felt a broken rib but no bullet.

Neither Bliss nor Townshend had washed their hands before touching the injury.

As the group of nine other doctors looked on, Bliss inserted an unsterilized metal probe about 3 inches (7.6 cm) into the wound. Again, Bliss failed to find the bullet. He thought it had gone downward into the abdominal area. Like Townshend, Bliss believed that the wound was fatal.

The hour of probing had been painful. Garfield was pale and covered with sweat. He asked to be moved to the White House, and the doctors agreed. He would get better care there than in a crowded hospital, which was generally for people with no one to nurse them at home.

A weekly newspaper's cover shows Garfield lying on the station floor. Without cameras to record Garfield's assassination, sketch artists created the images based on eyewitness accounts. Secretary Blaine is on the right. The matron of the ladies' waiting room cradles the president's head. One of his sons, eyes covered, stands over his father. Garfield's two oldest sons, who planned to accompany him on the train, entered the station moments after the shooting.

The president was carried on a mattress through the train station to the back of a horse-drawn ambulance for the short trip to the White House. Bliss and the group of doctors from the station followed.

Once there, the president was placed in bed on his right side so that the bloody discharge drained from the bullet hole more freely. No one cleaned or disinfected the wound before covering it with a temporary dressing. His bloody and dirty clothes would not be cut away until eight thirty that night.

Throughout the rest of the day, the doctors injected morphine to alleviate the pain in Garfield's legs. They gave him brandy and water. Every half hour he vomited, though he remained alert.

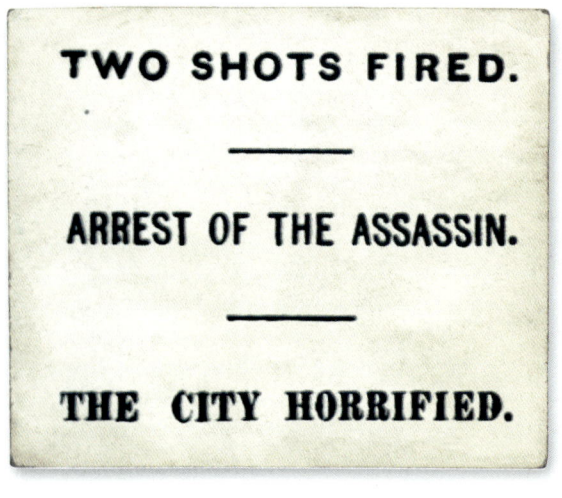

Headline from the Washington, DC, *Evening Star* on the day of the shooting

Later that evening, the president struggled to breathe. His heart raced. Bliss and the other doctors reconvened to discuss the case. Despite knowing it would be painful for Garfield, they decided they had to probe the wound again in order to learn more about his injury and determine how to handle it. The surgeon general of the U.S. Navy performed the exam by sticking his little finger into the bullet hole as far as he could. He told the others that he felt two fractured ribs and a cut in the liver.

A damaged liver would be fatal. In 1881, surgeons weren't able to safely repair injured organs or search for a bullet deep in the body. No one expected the president to survive the night.

THE BULLETINS

Starting hours after the shooting, the White House staff released the doctors' regular medical updates to the press. Garfield's secretary, Joseph

Stanley Brown, thought the public had a right to know what was happening with their president. The reporters' stories, sent by telegraph around the country, appeared in newspapers and on bulletin boards outside newspaper offices. According to most accounts, Garfield was doomed.

Yet by Sunday morning, the president's breathing and temperature had returned to normal. He wasn't out of danger, but he seemed better.

Later that day, Dr. Bliss dismissed the other physicians, explaining that it was best for Garfield if fewer doctors visited the sickroom. He had chosen his own permanent medical team. The team included Army Surgeon General Joseph Barnes and Dr. J. J. Woodward from the surgeon general's office. Neither doctor regularly treated patients. The third was Dr. Robert Reyburn, a surgeon and one of Bliss's friends. When anyone questioned Bliss's authority, he claimed that the Garfields asked him to supervise the president's care. Months later, Garfield's wife and physician cousin denied this.

Bliss took charge of the president's treatment and diet. The role of the rest of his team was to measure the patient's vital signs, keep records, take turns staying with him, and write bulletins to be released to the press two or three times daily. Confidently, Bliss told a reporter, "If I can't save him, no one can."

Although Bliss rejected assistance from any doctors other than his handpicked team, he sought advice from two nationally respected surgeons, Philadelphia's D. Hayes Agnew and New York's Frank Hamilton. On Monday morning, July 4, the two men arrived at the White House.

In examining Garfield's wound with probes, they failed to find the bullet's pathway past a broken rib. They guessed that it had gone downward into the pelvic region. Garfield was holding his own after two days, and the two surgeons believed that no organs had been damaged by the bullet. The president passed urine and feces normally, and neither contained blood. That meant that the kidneys and intestines were fine. Garfield wasn't paralyzed,

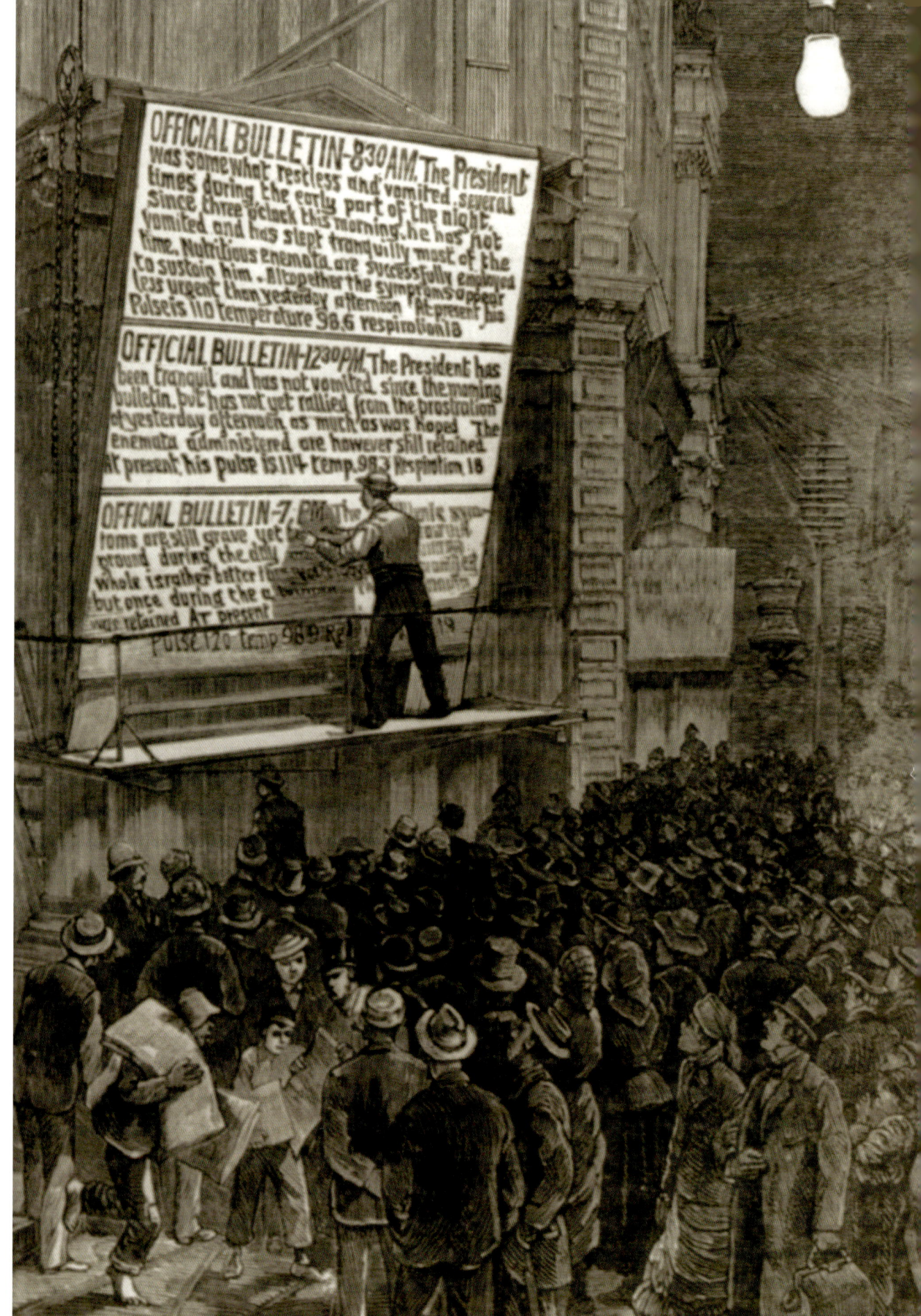

indicating that the spinal cord was intact. The discomfort in his feet and legs had likely been from temporary nerve injury. That pain gradually disappeared.

From their Civil War service and years of practice, Agnew and Hamilton knew that the body often encases a bullet in a cyst, or sac, making it harmless. As long as the bullet wasn't causing problems, they didn't think it wise to perform a risky operation to learn more.

Several days after the shooting, Garfield seemed much improved. Although bedridden, he was able to swallow chicken broth without vomiting, and he could sleep at night. Still, when the doctors changed his dressing twice a day, they saw pus seeping from the bullet wound. They weren't concerned. Like most American physicians, they thought pus was a sign that the body was healing.

But the daily bulletins about pus worried some outside doctors, especially younger ones. They were familiar with the recent writings of Dr. Joseph Lister, whose work in Scotland explained that pus was a sign of bacterial infection in a wound. Lister suspected that bacteria entered wounds on a surgeon's dirty hands and instruments, and he advised physicians to wash and sterilize both.

Two weeks after the shooting, Garfield was eating solid food. His wound continued to discharge pus, and he ran a slight temperature. Bliss and his medical team weren't troubled by it. They declared that the president was out of danger and would recover.

The evening bulletin on July 16 said, "The President has passed a better day than any since he was shot." The bulletin on July 21 reported that he was "doing excellently" and progressing well toward recovery. Based on

A crowd gathers by the bulletin board at the *New York Herald* where updates about Garfield's condition were posted several times a day.

that assessment, newspapers announced that Garfield would be out of bed in a couple of weeks. Garfield's family and close friends thought the crisis had passed.

THE CHANNEL OF PUS

Then on the morning of July 21, a small piece of clothing appeared in the pus draining from the wound. When Garfield was shot, the bullet had driven the cotton and wool fibers into his body. The next day, doctors found a tiny piece of rib bone and more fibers mixed with the pus. Bliss and his team informed Doctors Agnew and Hamilton that the wound was "looking very well" and "discharged several ounces of healthy pus." They seemed to consider this development good news.

On July 23, three weeks after the shooting, Garfield was not very well at all. He ran a high fever. He had sweats and intense chills. His heart raced. He vomited. The doctors recognized the symptoms of a severe infection overtaking Garfield's body. They alerted Agnew and Hamilton, who rushed to Washington.

The specialists found a pus-filled sac under the president's skin 3 inches (7.6 cm) below the bullet hole. They used a scalpel to open it and inserted a rubber tube so that the pus could better drain out.

The pus flowed, but within two days, Garfield redeveloped the high fever, sweating, chills, and vomiting. Agnew operated again to enlarge the opening and remove small pieces of bone from the wound, probably splintered off from the rib when the bullet struck. He put in two rubber tubes to drain the pus that filled a channel extending down from the bullet wound.

The medical bulletin on July 27 announced that Garfield was eating well again and feeling better. The "healthy" pus continued to flow. There was so much of it that a larger drainage tube had to be placed even deeper into the channel of pus. Yet the doctors continually reported in the bulletins that the wound looked good and Garfield was improving.

Actually, by early August, the president's condition was worsening. As his infection intensified, Garfield heavily perspired and ran a high fever. He couldn't eat without vomiting. The pus built up faster than it could drain out. Ultimately, the doctors were able to extend a flexible probe 12 inches (30.5 cm) from the bullet hole down the pus channel. Even as Garfield's health deteriorated, the White House staff sent out telegrams saying that the doctors believed he was better than at any time since July 2. Rumors to the contrary were untrue, they said.

All summer, the American people had paid close attention to the president's condition. Every morning they anxiously read the latest medical bulletin in their local newspaper. But despite the optimistic reports, the public wasn't getting the whole story. Dr. Reyburn later revealed that the bulletins were often intentionally misleading. He and the other doctors felt uncomfortable lying to the nation. Bliss, however, insisted on upbeat reports—even if they misrepresented the president's health. Bliss argued that Garfield would see the newspaper articles about him, and any negative information might discourage him and affect his recuperation.

The truth finally emerged by mid-August when reporters heard from insiders that the White House

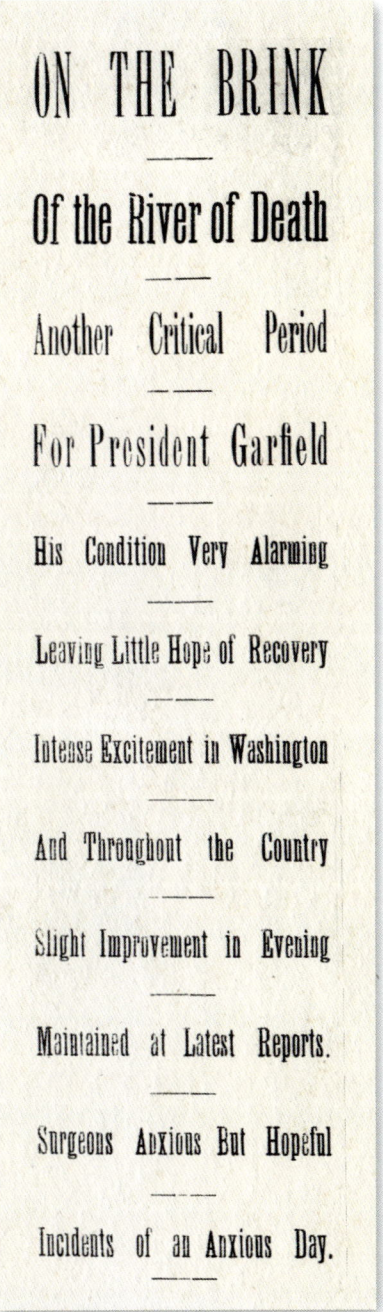

By mid-August, newspapers were reporting on Garfield's grave condition. The article that accompanied this headline from the *St. Paul* [MN] *Daily Globe* revealed that the mood in the White House is "a general feeling of anxiety and actual alarm."

President James Garfield was more than 6 feet tall (2 m) and weighed 210 pounds (95 kg) at the time of the shooting. He lost 80 pounds (36 kg) during the next eighty days.

was privately anxious and alarmed by Garfield's condition. He had developed abscesses the size of peas in his armpits and on his chest and back. The doctors cut them open, letting their bacteria-laden contents flow out. Fluid started to accumulate in Garfield's lungs. Infection had taken over his body.

By six weeks after the shooting, the president had lost nearly 80 pounds (36 kg). He had gone from being a robust and slightly overweight man to a skeletal figure. Visitors who saw him were shocked by his appearance. They came away convinced that he would never recover.

Medical journals and newspapers accused Bliss of mismanaging the president's care. In late August, one paper said, "The people of the United States never fully appreciated the force of the aphorism 'Ignorance is Bliss' until President Garfield was shot."

TO THE SEA

Garfield was weary and weak. He felt pain from the infected wound and the doctors' treatment of it. He wanted to be taken away from the depressing sickroom—to be outside, to see the sky, to gaze at the sea.

Deciding that the change might help him, the medical team agreed. On September 6, a special train transported the bedridden president, his doctors, his family, and his aides to Francklyn Cottage, a seaside home in Elberon, New Jersey. The refreshing, cool breezes and sound of breaking waves lifted Garfield's spirits.

Bliss continued to release medical bulletins that were falsely optimistic, saying on September 15 that Garfield "has made some progress towards convalescence." In reality, the president's body was rapidly failing. The lung infection worsened. He had chills followed by sweating. At times, he hallucinated.

Four days after Bliss's misleading bulletin, Garfield experienced a

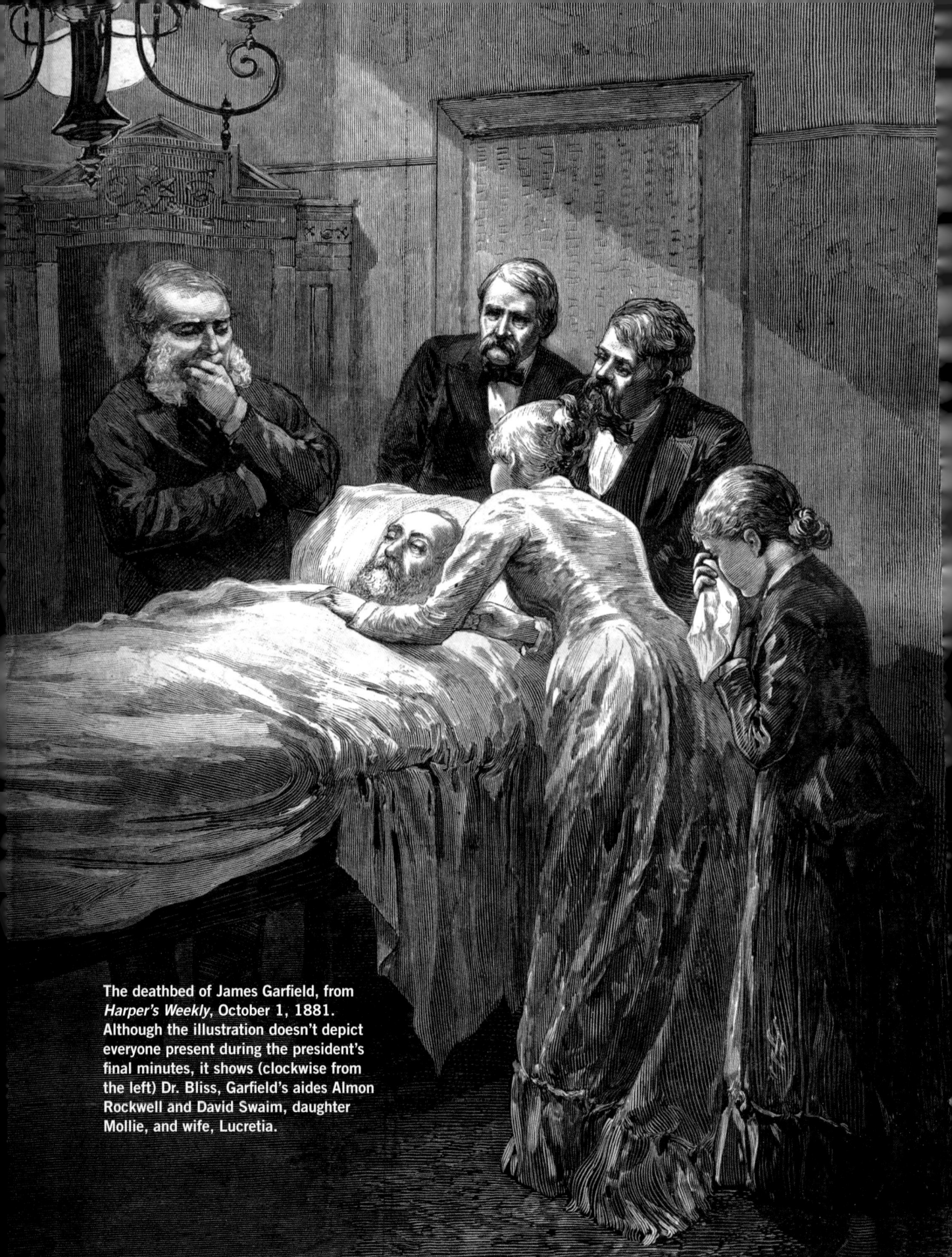

The deathbed of James Garfield, from *Harper's Weekly*, October 1, 1881. Although the illustration doesn't depict everyone present during the president's final minutes, it shows (clockwise from the left) Dr. Bliss, Garfield's aides Almon Rockwell and David Swaim, daughter Mollie, and wife, Lucretia.

coughing spell and intense chill, followed by profuse perspiration. He slept most of the day.

That evening, Garfield's aide David Swaim was on duty in the president's candlelit room. Shortly after ten p.m., he heard the president gasp. When he reached the bedside, Garfield opened his eyes.

"Oh my! Swaim, what a pain I have right here." The president placed his hand over his heart. Then he fell unconscious.

Swaim called for Dr. Bliss in the adjoining room. Soon others in the house rushed in and gathered around the bed.

Garfield's skin had lost all color. Bliss checked for a pulse at his wrist and neck. Nothing. He put his ear to the president's chest and heard a faint flutter.

"Mrs. Garfield," Dr. Bliss said to Lucretia, "the President is dying."

Lucretia tenderly kissed her husband's forehead and took his hand in hers.

While the solemn group waited, the president's gasps of breath continued for several more minutes until . . . silence. It was 10:35 p.m., September 19.

James Garfield was dead, eighty days after Charles Guiteau's bullet pierced his back.

THE MISSING BULLET

Garfield's body was taken by a funeral train back to Washington. Along the way, crowds stood silently at the black-draped rail stations. His casket lay in state in the U.S. Capitol Rotunda, where 100,000 mourners walked by to pay tribute. Later a train carried the casket to Ohio for a funeral and burial.

But before Garfield's body made the final trip away from Elberon, it revealed the answer to the question that doctors had asked since the moment the president fell to the floor at the Baltimore and Potomac Railroad Depot: Where was the bullet?

DEAD!

The President Died at 10:35 Last Night,

After Eighty Days of Intense Suffering.

He Passed Away in a Dream of His Old Home.

The Tolling of Bells and Demonstrations of Sorrow.

The Whole Country Mourns the Loss of James A. Garfield.

Vice-President Arthur Called to Take the Oath of Office

Strong Threats of Lynching Guiteau, the Assassin.

The headline from the *Las Vegas* [NV] *Daily Gazette*, September 20, 1881. Newspapers across the country carried similar announcements of Garfield's death.

On September 20, the afternoon after the president's death, Dr. Daniel Lamb of the U.S. Army Medical Museum performed an autopsy at Francklyn Cottage. Besides determining exactly what killed Garfield, the information would be needed as evidence in Charles Guiteau's murder trial.

Observing and assisting Lamb were the six doctors involved in Garfield's care. A local physician attended, too, because state law required a licensed New Jersey doctor to be present.

Several hours later, the doctors released a written summary of the autopsy to the press. The findings stunned nearly everyone. The bullet had not ended up in the lower abdomen where the doctors expected to find it. Its path through the body was not the channel of pus. Instead, after penetrating Garfield's skin to the right of his backbone, the bullet traveled downward and broke the two lowest ribs on his right side. Deflected to the left by the ribs, the bullet passed through the backbone, damaging bone and cartilage. But it did not strike Garfield's spinal cord. The temporary tingling in his feet and legs was likely from the initial impact to his backbone.

After exiting a vertebra, the bullet came to rest in fatty tissue behind the pancreas, a couple of inches to the left of the backbone. It lay there harmlessly for almost three months, becoming encased in a layer of scar tissue. None of Garfield's organs had been hit by the bullet.

According to the autopsy report, the channel of pus formed as result of infection caused by the tiny splintered bones broken off by the bullet. That infection entered the bloodstream and spread through Garfield's body, causing the chills and high fever that began three weeks after the shooting.

Lamb and the other doctors concluded that the bullet had grazed an artery near the pancreas. The torn edges of the artery's walls formed a sac that held blood flowing through the vessel. They blamed the president's death on the bursting of the sac. This proved that the bullet wound had been fatal from the beginning. Even if they'd known about its damage, it wasn't possible to do surgery to fix a blood vessel or remove a bullet deep in the body. Garfield was doomed to death from the moment the bullet struck him. There was nothing the doctors could have done to save his life.

NOT SO FAST

As soon as the autopsy results were published, members of the medical community challenged its conclusions.

Some critics argued that if the bullet had torn an artery, Garfield would have died right away. Several surgeons with gunshot wound experience alleged that the damage to Garfield's vertebrae and ribs wouldn't have caused the pus channel, a blood infection, or his death. Instead, the president's bullet wound had been contaminated with bacteria by his own doctors, starting with the first examination on the dirty floor of the railroad station.

Others said that there was nothing inevitable about Garfield's death. They charged that Bliss and his team were using the autopsy to exonerate themselves from errors in their care of the president. Bliss, in particular, seemed more concerned about protecting his reputation than admitting the obvious truth: The body of a forty-nine-year-old man in previous good health had been destroyed by infection and starvation.

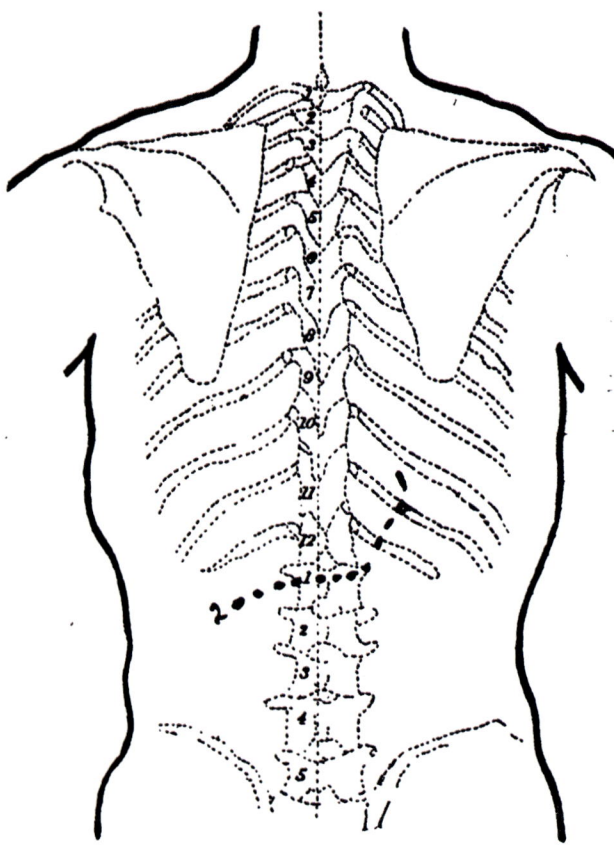

This drawing of Garfield's back shows the bullet's path starting at 1) where it entered his body, along the dotted line to 2) where it landed in fatty tissue. This illustration appeared in a book by Dr. Robert Reyburn, one of Garfield's doctors.

After more than one hundred and forty years, many modern medical experts who reviewed the record concluded that Garfield might have survived if his doctors had simply allowed his body to heal on its own. By futilely searching for the bullet with germ-laden fingers and probes, his physicians followed outdated medical ideas instead of Joseph Lister's antiseptic methods. Their mistakes led to a massive infection that the president's body couldn't fight.

AFTERMATH

Within two months of Garfield's death, Charles Guiteau was brought to trial for the intentional murder of the president. The prosecution detailed how Guiteau had bought his gun and stalked Garfield with the intent of killing him. Doctors Bliss, Barnes, Woodward, and Lamb all testified that the bullet wound had been a mortal one from which Garfield couldn't have recovered. They stood by the autopsy's results.

Guiteau's attorney argued that his client was insane. For that reason, he shouldn't be held responsible for his actions. Without his lawyer's blessing, Guiteau announced to the crowded courtroom, "I deny the killing . . . we admit the shooting." He blamed Garfield's doctors. "His death was caused by malpractice. That is all there is to it."

The jury disagreed. On January 25, 1882, the twelve-man panel took less than an hour to find the defendant guilty of premeditated murder. The judge's sentence of hanging was carried out on June 30, 1882, two days before the shooting's one-year anniversary.

The constant publicity about the assassination throughout the summer of 1881, the doctors' controversial care, and Garfield's ultimate death shined the light on the role of microbes in human health. By the last decade of the nineteenth century, America's physicians embraced Joseph Lister's recommendations. Ordinary people were aware of the importance of cleanliness in preventing infection.

Although President James Garfield didn't benefit from these changes, the tragic fiasco leading to his death helped propel the American medical community into the twentieth century.

CHESTER ARTHUR

21st PRESIDENT

BORN: October 5, 1829, in Fairfield, Vermont

PROFESSION BEFORE PRESIDENCY: teacher, principal, lawyer, customs collector at the Port of New York

POLITICAL PARTY: Republican

ELECTED: vice president in 1880

SERVED: September 1881 (upon President Garfield's death) to March 1885

DIED: November 18, 1886, in New York, New York, age fifty-seven

PRESIDENTIAL TRIVIA:

★ Arthur was the third president to serve in a single year, 1881. Rutherford Hayes finished his term on March 3. James Garfield was inaugurated March 4. Arthur succeeded to the presidency on September 20 after Garfield's death

★ Because Arthur's wife died before he became president, he had no first lady. His youngest sister took over the role as White House hostess.

Chester Alan Arthur in 1882, his first full year as president

CHAPTER TWO

THE HIDDEN DIAGNOSIS

"I have not been sick at all."
—CHESTER ARTHUR

THE UNLIKELY VICE PRESIDENT

CHESTER ARTHUR DIDN'T PLAN TO BE PRESIDENT. IT HAD NEVER BEEN HIS ambition. But late on the night of September 19, 1881, the sound of Manhattan's tolling bells alerted him that the weight of that office would soon be on his shoulders.

Arthur was born in Vermont, one of a Baptist minister's nine children. After graduating from Union College in Schenectady, New York, Arthur taught school in a small town in Vermont, where he later served as principal. By the time he was in his early twenties, he had studied law and begun working as an attorney in New York City. Soon after, he became active in the Republican Party, eventually rising to be the close friend and associate of Senator Roscoe Conkling, a leading New York Republican politician.

That connection helped to make Arthur a wealthy man. During President Ulysses Grant's administration, Arthur served as collector of customs at the Port of New York, thanks to a political appointment arranged by Conkling. The majority of imported goods came into the United States through New York City's port. The Customs House collected tens of millions of dollars in duties on these products, and this money made up a large part of the U.S. government's income. Arthur's collector position gave him—and Conkling—the power to hand out hundreds of well-paying jobs to loyal friends and supporters.

Arthur was the highest-paid federal employee. He had a reputation as a rich gentleman who lived in a fancy house, had a personal valet, and ate in expensive restaurants. He was known for his sense of style and fashion. Some said he owned more than seventy pairs of trousers.

The next president, Rutherford Hayes, tried to reform the spoils system that rewarded favors with government appointments. During his administration, he defied Conkling and replaced Arthur, though Arthur was never directly accused of corruption.

When Hayes decided not to run for a second term, Republicans chose James Garfield as their 1880 presidential candidate. Arthur was added to the ticket as the vice president despite never holding an elected office. He was picked for only one reason: He was close to Conkling, a man whose support Garfield needed in order to win election. Otherwise, Conkling was unlikely to back Garfield.

At the time of his nomination, Arthur was practicing law in New York City. He had faced tragedy just five months before his name was put on the Republican ticket. His beloved wife, Ellen, died suddenly of pneumonia, leaving him with a fifteen-year-old son and an eight-year-old daughter. Arthur took her death hard. From then on, he placed a bouquet of flowers by her photograph every day.

In November 1880, the Garfield–Arthur ticket was victorious at the polls, and on March 4 the two men took their oaths of office in Washington. Afterward, Arthur remained close to Roscoe Conkling, even living with the senator in Washington. But he had little contact with Garfield or his allies, who he knew didn't trust him.

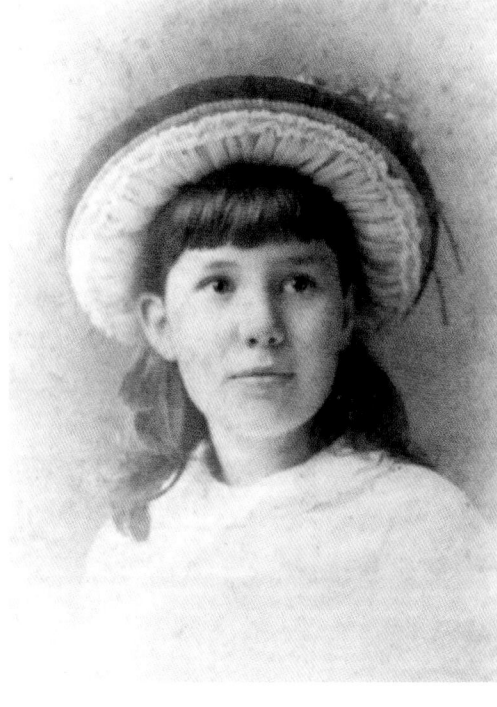

Chester Arthur's daughter, Nell, was almost ten when her father became president.

Then on July 2, just four months after Inauguration Day, Charles Guiteau shot a bullet into President James Garfield's back.

Writings found in Guiteau's pocket after his arrest indicated that his motive for shooting Garfield was to put the vice president in power. "I expect President Arthur and Senator Conkling will give the Nation the finest administration it has ever had," said one of the letters.

Within hours of Guiteau's attack, rumors spread, accusing Arthur of participating in the plot to kill Garfield. Arthur had been shocked by the shooting and knew nothing about it beforehand. But the allegation cast a shadow on him. Arthur released public statements condemning the shooting. He denied associating with Guiteau other than occasionally seeing him at New York City's Republican headquarters during the 1880 presidential campaign.

As Garfield struggled for his life, Arthur prayed that he would survive. He didn't want the presidency, certainly not this way. Many Americans worried that Chester Arthur might indeed become president. They questioned his ability and experience. He gave the impression that he was more qualified to throw a party than to run the country. They had voted for Garfield, never anticipating that Arthur might inherit the office.

One influential New York leader who knew Arthur wrote later that when he heard of Garfield's assassination, his first reaction was shock that Arthur might take over. "It was a common saying of that time among those who knew him best, 'Chet Arthur President of the United States! Good God!'"

Others were alarmed by the idea that Arthur, a man who had been part of the corrupt political machine of Roscoe Conkling, could be the next chief executive. Former President Rutherford Hayes expressed his dread in his diary: "The death of the President at this time would be a national calamity. . . . Arthur for President! Conkling the power behind the throne, superior to the throne!"

THE WORST NEWS

Throughout the summer of 1881, Arthur kept a low profile at his New York City home while Garfield lay suffering in bed. The White House sent him the doctors' daily bulletins, but Arthur never saw Garfield during the president's entire ordeal.

When Garfield didn't recover as hoped, rumblings came from the press and others that he was too incapacitated to serve. The cabinet raised this issue with Arthur and suggested he assume Garfield's responsibilities. Arthur refused to discuss it.

But Chester Arthur was soon forced to accept his new place in history. On Monday morning, September 19, Garfield's cabinet sent word to Arthur at his Manhattan home, alerting him that the president was close to death. Later that evening, Arthur realized that the end had come. By midnight, church bells were already ringing in mourning, and reporters had converged on the sidewalk outside Arthur's house.

Chester Arthur takes the oath of office in his New York City home early in the morning of September 20, 1881. Witnesses included his seventeen-year-old son, Alan, who stands behind his father.

Around 12:30 a.m., the cabinet's official telegram arrived. It informed Arthur that Garfield had died about two hours earlier. The vice president should take the oath of office immediately.

At 2:15 on the morning of September 20, 1881, Arthur and several witnesses gathered in his parlor at 123 Lexington Avenue. The group included his seventeen-year-old son, Alan. A judge, awakened from his sleep, administered the oath, and Chester Alan Arthur became the twenty-first president. Two days later, he traveled to Washington for a short public ceremony at the Capitol where the U.S. Supreme Court's chief justice formally swore him in.

A single bullet had changed his future, and faulty medical care by James Garfield's doctors had sealed Arthur's fate. He hadn't sought the presidency. But now that it was thrust upon him, Arthur tried to do his best for the country. He was aware of the challenges ahead after the trauma of Garfield's slow death. The *New York Times* commented the day after he took his oath, "No man ever assumed the Presidency of the United States under more trying circumstances."

Arthur didn't move into the White House right away. Upon inspecting the Executive Mansion, he saw that it needed a major upgrade. When President Garfield was shot, the Garfields had been in the process of redecorating the building and replacing some of the furniture. The renovations, which had been approved by Congress, remained incomplete. Building materials lay where workers had left them when Garfield died.

This cover of a weekly satirical magazine comments on "Chet" Arthur moving out of the White House during the summer of 1882 so that several rooms could be renovated. During that period, the president took fishing vacations, including one to New York's Thousand Islands.

VOL 2.

Nº 49

THE JUDGE.

ENTERED AT THE POST OFFICE AT NEW YORK AS SECOND CLASS MATTER COPYRIGHT 1881 BY THE JUDGE PUBLISHING CO.

Price   NEW YORK, SEPTEMBER 30, 1882.   10 Cents

RETURN OF "CHET" TO BUSINESS AGAIN.

A VERY SUCCESSFUL VACATION.

Arthur set up his residence and office in the home of a senator near the Capitol. He stayed there for three months. He ordered the renovation work resumed, and he monitored the progress himself. The unsanitary and broken plumbing was repaired. Bathrooms and an elevator were added. Arthur replaced furniture and carpets, auctioning off twenty-four wagons full of furnishings that he decided were out-of-date or worn out. The next year, he hired the famous New York City designer Louis Comfort Tiffany to renovate several rooms.

The president brought his taste for elegance to the White House in entertaining, too, and he frequently held dinners and receptions in the renovated mansion. As a widower, he had no first lady to act as hostess. He asked his youngest sister, Mary Arthur McElroy, to move into the White House and fill that role during part of the year. She brought her two daughters and also took care of Arthur's young daughter, Nell.

Arthur pleasantly surprised his doubters by upholding the dignity of the presidency and by breaking away from the influence of the Roscoe Conkling and his followers.

THE SECRET

According to presidential observers, Arthur wasn't as industrious as Garfield or his other predecessors had been. He typically came to his office after ten in the morning, took long lunches, and quit work by five in the afternoon. White House staff complained that Arthur procrastinated about completing important tasks.

But all was not what it seemed. Arthur had been considered hardworking when he was an attorney and the collector of customs. He was described as energetic during the 1880 campaign. His apparent laziness as president had another explanation.

PROBABLE EFFECT OF HAVING A DUDE PRESIDENT.

PRESIDENT ARTHUR IS VERY FASTIDIOUS ABOUT HIS CLOTHES, AND IS ONE OF THE BEST-DRESSED MEN IN THE COUNTRY.—*Daily Paper.*

This cartoon appeared on May 9, 1883, in *Puck* magazine. It makes fun of Chester Arthur's fashionable wardrobe. Arthur was 6 feet 2 inches tall (about 2 m) and had distinctive sideburns.

Hints of trouble appeared less than a year after Arthur became president. During the summer of 1882, his physician cousin stayed in the White House and noticed that Arthur was often ill and cranky. Then in early October 1882, a press story claimed that Arthur had been diagnosed with Bright's disease by the U.S. surgeon general. According to reports, a New York specialist was brought in to consult, and he agreed with that diagnosis. Arthur was advised to rest.

Bright's disease was the nineteenth-century term for a serious kidney ailment known today as nephritis. In this condition, the kidneys are inflamed and no longer filter the blood effectively. Symptoms include blood in the urine, high blood pressure, fatigue, and swelling in the feet, hands, abdomen, and face. The illness wasn't well understood in 1882. Treatments then included warm baths, opium, mercury, laxatives, and a diet that avoided alcohol, red meat, and cheese.

In a statement to the newspapers, the White House denied reports of Arthur's illness. "Any stories of the President's having chronic disease of any kind are pure fabrications," it declared. The statement went on to say that Arthur had no kidney ailments of which he was aware. He'd had a cold at one point. And he'd been bothered by malaria recently—not uncommon in mosquito-plagued Washington—but it had been a mild case. His doctors had recommended that he go inland to recover from that, which was the reason he took a September trip to the Thousand Islands in New York State. Now he was fully recovered.

It wasn't true. The president was so fatigued that he couldn't work a full day. He *was* aware that he had Bright's disease, that it was incurable, and that it would ultimately kill him.

Arthur continued to keep his illness a secret. The country had just dealt with Garfield's slow death. Arthur was reluctant to add his failing health to the public's anxiety. Even though he didn't know how long he had to live, he was considering a run for president in 1884. News of this ailment would end any chance of receiving his party's nomination.

Still, some people noticed that Arthur wasn't himself. In January 1883, he visited New York City, and those who saw him commented that he looked frail.

Under the headline, "The President Not Well," a *New York Times* article on March 11, 1883, reported that Arthur "has been far from well for several weeks," due to a bad cold that he couldn't shake. On the same day, Arthur wrote to his son that he'd been too ill to do the work required of him as president.

DENIALS

Explaining that a warmer climate would help him recover from his cold, Arthur planned a fishing trip to Florida. On April 5, 1883, he left Washington by train and took along Secretary of the Navy William Chandler, his personal secretary, a New York City friend, his valet, and a chef. Four reporters were allowed to accompany the group, and they filed reports as the trip progressed.

In Jacksonville, Florida, they all boarded a boat to go up the St. Johns River. The weather was hot. The mosquitoes were annoying. Arthur's health worsened. The reporters wrote that he was irritable and often angry, and his face was sunburned.

By April 18, the travelers had returned to the coast and boarded a ship that carried them north to Savannah, Georgia. On the day they arrived there, Arthur was busy with formal receptions in the city. During a long carriage ride, he was exposed to the blistering sun. He didn't return to the ship and his bed until midnight.

At 2:30 a.m., Arthur awoke with excruciating abdominal pain, chills, and a cold sweat. He cried out for his valet, who then fetched the ship's

VOL. 5.

NO. 120.

THE JUDGE.

ENTERED AT THE POST OFFICE AT NEW YORK AS SECOND CLASS MATTER. COPYRIGHT 1881 BY THE JUDGE PUBLISHING CO.

Price

NEW YORK, FEBRUARY 2, 1884.

10 Cents.

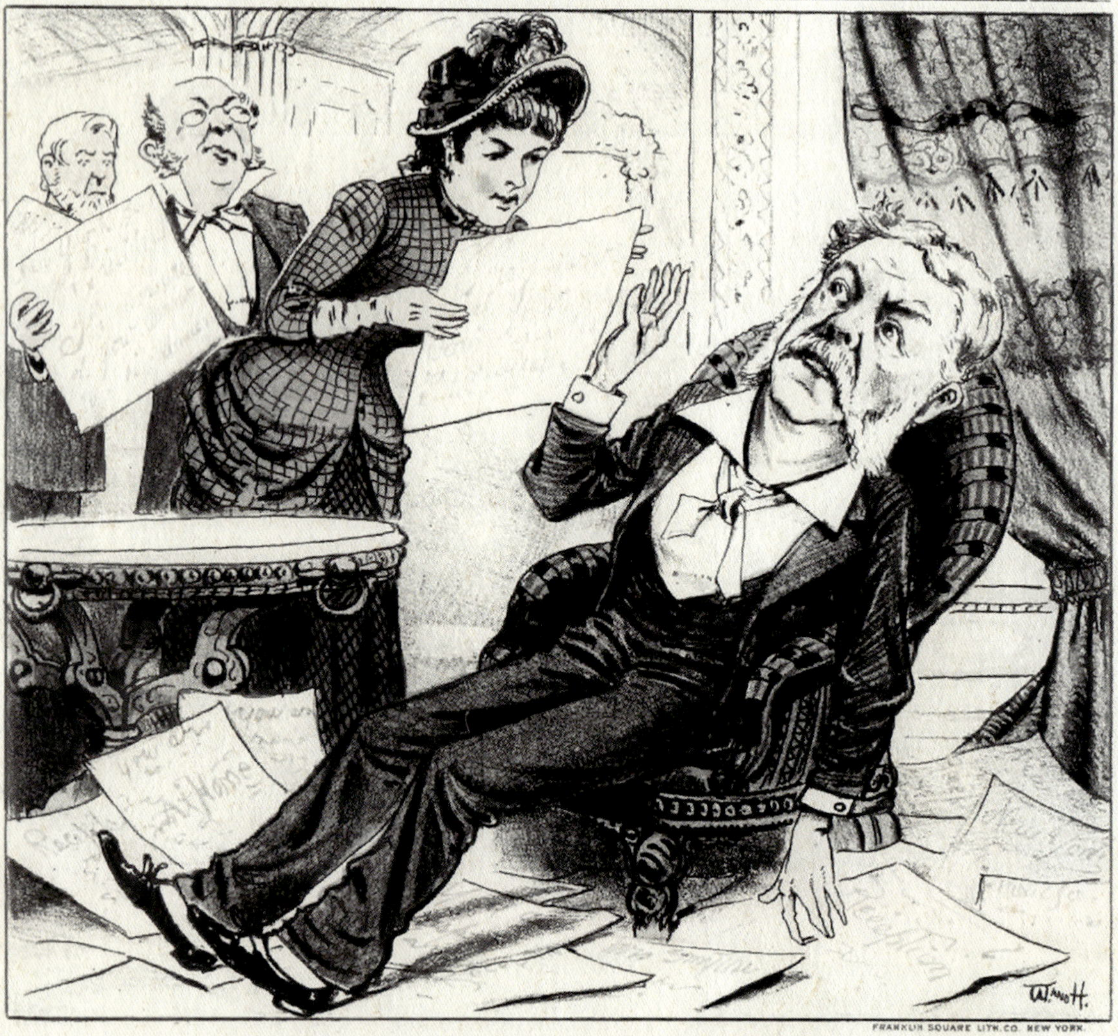

OUR SICK PRESIDENT.

Too much Sociability, and not enough Business.

doctor. Swearing Dr. Clarence Black to secrecy, Arthur told him about his kidney disease. Years later, Black reported that the president was critically ill that night.

The doctor put hot towels onto the president's body and gave him a sedative. After a couple of hours, Arthur seemed better. He spent the next day in bed and decided to return to Washington quickly, by train rather than by ship as originally planned.

Because reporters were along for the trip, news of Arthur's medical scare leaked. Maintaining his pledge to hide the truth, Dr. Black told the press that the incident was simply the result of too much sun exposure and some indigestion due to seasickness. The president's travel companions downplayed the event. Accounts of it appeared in major newspapers anyway.

On the nearly two-day-long train journey back to Washington, Arthur felt ill and weak. But he was determined to hide it when he arrived. There had already been too much speculation about his health.

When the train pulled into Washington on the night of April 22, about 200 people met it, including Arthur's son and several cabinet members. They'd read the press reports about his attack in Savannah, and they were concerned.

Arthur stepped off the train, smiling and appearing relaxed. Reporters at the station noted that he looked tanned and healthy.

"How are you feeling?" asked one of his friends.

"I haven't been sick a day," replied the president. "I've enjoyed the trip very much."

This magazine cover from the February 2, 1884, issue of *Judge* hints at Arthur's reputation of enjoying parties more than work. Although the White House always denied that Arthur was seriously ill, he had suffered several publicized episodes of sickness. Rumors that he had Bright's disease turned out to be true.

In August 1883, Arthur traveled to Yellowstone National Park. Seated in the middle, he poses with several traveling companions. Despite Arthur's attempt to appear vigorous, the trip strained his health.

A reporter at the station inquired further by interviewing Secretary of the Navy Chandler, Arthur's travel companion. Chandler denied that Arthur had been seriously ill. He said that the episode at Savannah was caused by "a long ride in the hot sun; but it [the episode] lasted only a few hours." In fact, said Chandler, the trip had rejuvenated Arthur. He went on to condemn the reporters who had written about the chills and pain. "Their sensational dispatches about the President's sickness were unjustifiable."

Arthur's private secretary, who had also been on the trip, went out of his way to speak to a reporter. He stated that it was a false rumor that Arthur had had malaria chills and needed a doctor. The president had merely experienced "a slight attack of indigestion."

The secretary of state had come to the station to greet the president.

He also told a reporter that Arthur's health was good with the exception of "a slight attack of indigestion."

Chester Arthur and his inner circle had deceived the public. Despite their coordinated lies, Arthur wasn't getting any better.

In the late summer of 1883, he took another vacation, this time to Yellowstone National Park in Wyoming. The refreshing mountain air and period away from the job failed to revive him. When Arthur returned to Washington on September 7, he announced that he was in perfect health. But in private, he saw a doctor about his pain and swollen legs, side effects of Bright's disease. The physician told him to take on a lighter workload, eat a better diet, and get more sleep.

Nothing helped. During the rest of his term, Arthur suffered from pain and fatigue. He continued to pretend that he was strong and well. Unlike previous presidents, however, he avoided press interviews and refused to answer questions about his personal life, including his health. Only a few close friends, including his secretary of state, knew the truth. They didn't reveal the secret.

A SECOND TERM?

Arthur's time in office was unremarkable. He had no major crises to handle such as war or economic depression.

He was best known for signing the Pendleton Civil Service Reform Act in January 1883. This had been proposed several years before by those who wanted to end the system of hiring government employees based on their political connections. Garfield's assassination by a disgruntled job seeker spurred the public into demanding an end to the spoils system, and the reformers gained enough votes in Congress to pass a bill. Early in his term, Arthur encouraged Congress to approve it, even though he had benefited from the spoils system as collector at the Port of New York. The Act established the first examinations required to fill some federal government jobs.

As the 1884 presidential election approached, Arthur was half-hearted in competing for his party's nomination, perhaps because of his illness. He even asked his cabinet members not to go to the Republican Party's nominating convention in June 1884 to support him.

Arthur had disappointed one branch of the party when he cut ties with Roscoe Conkling and turned against the people who thrived under the spoils system. He'd never impressed the other Republicans. At the convention, the delegates chose James Blaine, who had been Garfield's secretary of state. In the November 1884 general election, Blaine was defeated by Democrat Grover Cleveland. (See chapter three.) It was the first presidential election the Republicans had lost in twenty-four years.

At the end of his term in March 1885, Arthur planned to practice law at his old New York firm. But his health had deteriorated. He was often too sick to go to the office and rarely went out in public. Eventually, he developed advanced heart disease as a consequence of his kidney problems. He lost weight and became extremely weak. By his fifty-seventh birthday in early October 1886, Arthur could no longer get out of bed.

On November 16, he told his son and an old friend to get rid of his official and personal papers. They burned them as Arthur requested.

Two days later, at five in the morning, Chester Arthur died of a stroke, less than two years after he retired from the presidency. He was buried beside his wife in the family plot at Albany Rural Cemetery in Menands, New York.

Since October 1882, a year into Arthur's presidential term, some newspapers had periodically reported that he suffered from Bright's disease. Every time, Arthur and those close to him vehemently denied it. The press accounts were never confirmed until the day of his death when

his personal doctor announced that the former president had had Bright's disease. The physician also reported that Arthur's heart had been enlarged and weakened for two or three years. "His great physical strength pulled him through as far as this," he said.

Arthur was remembered as a man who surprised the nation by the way he handled his office. After his death, the *New York Times* said of him: "He was one of the few Presidents of recent times who left the office in higher esteem and reputation than he enjoyed when he entered upon it."

While he was president, Arthur denied reports of his illness. His well-publicized outdoor activities like camping and fishing gave the impression that he was healthy and hardy.

"No man ever entered the Presidency so profoundly and widely distrusted as Chester Alan Arthur," said one writer, "and no one ever retired from that highest civil trust of the world more generally respected, alike by political friend and foe."

Yet Chester Arthur had hidden a dark, significant secret from most of his cabinet, from Congress, and from the public. Throughout his three and a half years in office, he had no vice president. What if he had died from his incurable disease earlier than he did?

According to a law passed in 1792, the next in line would have been the president pro tempore of the Senate followed by the speaker of the House

Chester Arthur's gravesite in Albany Rural Cemetery, Menands, New York. In June 1889, nearly three years after his death, Arthur's friends paid for this monument consisting of a black granite sarcophagus and bronze Angel of Sorrow.

of Representatives. But for several weeks after Arthur took office in 1881, these two positions were unfilled. The law listed no other positions in the line of succession.

To prevent this potential crisis from happening again, Congress passed the Presidential Succession Act of 1886. The law added more officials to the line of succession. After the vice president came the cabinet officers, starting with the secretary of state. The speaker of the House and president pro tempore of the Senate were taken out of the line.

Arthur's term raised another question about presidential succession: What happens if a president is unable to carry out his duties? While James Garfield was slowly dying during the summer of 1881, no one was sure what to do about transferring power to his vice president. Once Arthur became president, he raised the question of presidential disability with Congress. He called on the legislators to fix the Constitution's vagueness about what defines a president's inability to govern; who decides when the vice president should take over; and whether the vice president has to hand back power if the president recovers.

Congress failed to act for more than eighty years.

GROVER CLEVELAND

22nd and 24th PRESIDENT

BORN: March 18, 1837, in Caldwell, New Jersey

PROFESSION BEFORE PRESIDENCY: lawyer, county sheriff, mayor, governor

POLITICAL PARTY: Democrat

ELECTED: 1884 and 1892

SERVED: March 1885 to March 1889 and March 1893 to March 1897

DIED: June 24, 1908, in Princeton, New Jersey, age seventy-one

PRESIDENTIAL TRIVIA:

★ Cleveland rose from mayor of Buffalo, New York, to the state's governor, to president in just three years.

★ He was the only president to get married in the White House. On his wedding day, June 2, 1886, Cleveland was forty-nine; his bride was twenty-seven years younger. His daughter was the only presidential child born in the White House (on September 9, 1893).

Stephen Grover Cleveland in 1892, the year he was elected president for the second time. (Cleveland didn't use his given first name.)

CHAPTER THREE

THE VANISHING PRESIDENT

"Whatever you do, tell the truth."
—GROVER CLEVELAND

A SUSPICIOUS SORE

BY EARLY MAY 1893, FIFTY-SIX-YEAR-OLD GROVER CLEVELAND HAD BEEN president for two months. The job wasn't new to him, though. He had already served one four-year term as the nation's chief executive.

But Cleveland soon learned that things had changed since he left the White House in March 1889. The country faced economic disaster. This period was known as the Panic of 1893, and it was one of the most serious economic crises in American history. Hundreds of banks closed down. Dozens of railroads went bankrupt. Businesses laid off workers or shuttered forever. Millions of people were unemployed.

As if Cleveland didn't have enough to concern him, on the morning of May 5, he felt a tender area on the roof of his mouth. Over the next several weeks, the sore became more annoying, even painful. Finally on Sunday, June 18, Cleveland asked Dr. Robert O'Reilly to take a look. O'Reilly, a U.S. Army doctor, was responsible for attending the president.

O'Reilly didn't like the look of the quarter-sized ulcer. He asked a dentist to check whether the sore was related to the president's teeth. No, the dentist said, it wasn't a dental problem. To learn more, O'Reilly scraped some tissue from the rough surface and sent the sample to a pathologist at the Army Medical Museum in Washington. He labeled the samples with a fictious name to maintain Cleveland's privacy.

When the results came back, the news wasn't good. The pathologist couldn't be absolutely sure, but under the microscope the tissue sample looked like oral cancer. O'Reilly realized the president would need surgery to remove the cancerous area. It was impossible to predict how dire this affliction might be.

Cleveland's wife, Frances, had been concerned about the sore, too. After O'Reilly's preliminary diagnosis, she wrote to Dr. Joseph Bryant. Bryant had been the family's personal doctor when the Clevelands lived in New York City between his two terms. She arranged to meet Bryant when she traveled through New York the next day on her way to Gray Gables, the family's summer home on Cape Cod, Massachusetts.

The June 1886 wedding of President Grover Cleveland and Frances Folsom held in the White House Blue Room. This illustration appeared in *Harper's Weekly*, June 12, 1886.

Bryant was a renowned surgeon, and Frances and her husband trusted his advice. She was seven months pregnant with their second child, and she used that as a cover for the meeting to avoid raising questions among the press.

After Bryant heard Mrs. Cleveland's description of the sore, he took the train to Washington to examine the president himself. He concurred with O'Reilly's diagnosis. Bryant sent another sample of the sore to a respected pathologist at Johns Hopkins University, who confirmed that it was probably cancerous.

"Were it in my mouth," Bryant told Cleveland, "I would have it removed at once."

The president agreed to the surgery.

KEEPING THE SECRET

Any cancer diagnosis was dreaded in the days long before effective chemotherapy and radiation treatments. Eight years earlier, former President Ulysses Grant had died from throat cancer, and his suffering had been widely publicized. Cleveland knew people would remember Grant when they heard about his own cancer. It was important that Americans saw their president as vigorous and in control. The news that his life was in mortal danger would send shock waves through the country and likely exacerbate the economic crisis. No one must know about this diagnosis.

Dr. Bryant assembled a medical team to assist him in removing the cancer. Several of the doctors practiced in New York City, including Edward G. Janeway, an accomplished surgeon who would monitor the president's vital signs; John Erdmann, a young surgeon who worked with Bryant; and Ferdinand Hasbrouck, a dentist skilled in extracting teeth and an expert at using nitrous oxide (laughing gas) to anesthetize patients. Dr. O'Reilly would administer ether as an anesthetic if the nitrous oxide didn't keep the president asleep during the operation. Finally, Bryant asked W. W. Keen, a nationally known and respected surgeon from Philadelphia, to help him with the procedure itself. The group was told not to disclose anything about the assignment, even to family.

Cleveland and his close friend Secretary of War Daniel Lamont decided that the operation, like the cancer diagnosis, would have to be kept secret. That ruled out performing the surgery at the White House or in a hospital where the press might find out. Instead, they asked banker Elias Benedict, Cleveland's friend from New York City, if they could use his yacht. As it sailed far offshore, no one would be able to see what was happening onboard. Cleveland and Benedict often fished together from the yacht, so the president's presence on the *Oneida* wouldn't raise suspicions.

In 1893, it wasn't unusual for a president to leave hot, humid Washington during the summer. Congress usually adjourned for the season, too. No one was surprised when Lamont informed the press that Cleveland would be sailing on Benedict's yacht to Gray Gables at Buzzards Bay.

On Friday afternoon, June 30, President Cleveland and Lamont left Washington in a private railcar. By late evening, they had arrived in the New York City area and were spotted by several reporters. Cleveland curtly told them that he was going to his summer home for a rest. He had nothing else to say.

After meeting up with Dr. Bryant in Manhattan, the men boarded a small boat at a pier on the East River, and it took them to the anchored *Oneida*. The other doctors had already arrived separately to avoid alerting the press, carrying their surgical equipment in their baggage. The yacht's crew thought the president was having some routine dental work done in the privacy and pleasant surroundings of the yacht.

That evening, Cleveland relaxed on the *Oneida*, smoking a cigar and casually talking to the men who would be cutting into his head the next day.

THE FLOATING OPERATING ROOM

Despite making careful plans and gathering skilled doctors, Bryant worried about something going wrong. The operation was risky even when it wasn't done on a moving boat. Earlier in his career, Bryant had studied the procedure and discovered that as many as 14 percent of patients died from bleeding. Although he was an experienced surgeon, he had only performed this particular operation twice himself.

To complicate the situation, Grover Cleveland was a poor candidate for surgery. He was obese, smoked cigars, drank alcohol, and rarely exercised. He also had gout, a condition which was often the result of obesity, alcohol use, and a diet high in red meats and seafood. His gout caused painful joints that sometimes made Cleveland walk with a limp. What would be the repercussions if the president died during the procedure from the shock to his heart? Or if blood clots formed after the operation, killing him? Uneasily, Dr. Bryant commented to the *Oneida*'s captain, "If you hit a rock, hit it good and hard, so that we'll all go to the bottom!"

The next morning, the yacht slowly headed up the East River and into Long Island Sound, powered by its steam engine. The water was calm.

Around noon on Saturday, July 1, Cleveland entered the yacht's salon, or living room, and sat down in a large chair with his head leaned back and steadied by pillows. He would stay in this position throughout the surgery. The president showed no signs of nervousness despite knowing the potential danger ahead.

Unlike the doctors who cared for James Garfield in 1881, the team washed their hands and sterilized their surgical equipment. Both the room and Cleveland's mouth had been disinfected. A half hour later, the surgeons were ready to start.

THE PRESS ASKS QUESTIONS

Cleveland's initial recovery went well without complications, and he was on his feet by late July 3. The yacht sailed on, making stops along the route to Cape Cod to drop off the assisting surgeons. Late on the night of Wednesday, July 5, Cleveland, Bryant, and Lamont got off at Gray Gables on Buzzards Bay, unseen by the press.

A small group of reporters had been staying nearby, waiting for the president. Because the yacht trip from New York to Buzzards Bay typically took about fifteen hours, they wondered where he'd been for the past several days. He'd even missed the Fourth of July celebrations. When they heard on the morning of July 6 that Cleveland had slipped into Gray Gables during the night, they realized they'd been tricked. They wanted an explanation.

Secretary of War Daniel Lamont took charge of handling the press. Later that day he explained that there was no reason to make a big deal of Cleveland's absence. The president had enjoyed a slow, relaxing journey to Buzzards Bay. He was in fine health except for a flare-up of rheumatism that would require him to get total rest through the month of July. Cleveland was known to have occasional rheumatism, likely the result of gout.

But the next day, several newspapers across the country ran stories about Cleveland having had a cancerous growth successfully removed from his mouth while he was on the yacht. Headlines read: "Had He a Cancer?" and "Cleveland Ill." The articles acknowledged that this could be a rumor, though "the report is accepted as having some basis of truth." After all, Cleveland had been fine when he left Washington on June 30. He had been gone a long time, and now Lamont was saying that he would be incapacitated for a month.

The revelation led additional newspapers to send reporters to Gray Gables to investigate.

Bryant and Lamont weren't sure where the press heard about the cancer. Someone who participated in the surgery must have talked, and Bryant had his suspicions about who that was. The two men were quick to quash the story. When a reporter asked Bryant about Cleveland's health, the doctor responded, "The President is all right and only suffering from rheumatism."

On Friday evening, July 7, Lamont met with the reporters far enough from the Gray Gables house that no one would catch a telltale glimpse of the recovering Cleveland. Lamont told the group that the president needed dental work, and it was more comfortable to have it done on the yacht. Any other version they heard was just fabricated rumors by Cleveland's political opponents.

To back this up, Lamont made public a message he'd sent to Secretary of State Walter Gresham in which he said there was no basis for thinking that Cleveland had mouth cancer. "The president is laid up with rheumatism in his knee and foot," wrote Lamont, "and will be out in a day or two."

Lamont enlisted the help of one of Cleveland's friends and neighbors at Buzzards Bay, the actor Joseph Jefferson. Claiming to have visited Gray Gables on Friday, July 7, Jefferson announced to the press that Cleveland "has much improved in health and is very cheerful." It was a lie. Jefferson likely never saw Cleveland.

Frances Cleveland even spoke to reporters and asked them to stop spreading rumors about her husband.

On Saturday, July 8, Attorney General Richard Olney visited Gray Gables to work on presidential business with Cleveland. No one had informed him of the surgery, though he saw right away that the president's appearance had drastically changed. Cleveland had lost weight, and his mouth was so filled with wads of gauze that his speech was barely understandable.

"My God, Olney, they nearly killed me!" mumbled the president.

The attorney general came away believing that the president expected to die. Olney was instructed to lie about Cleveland's condition, if asked. And he *was* asked by still-curious reporters who hadn't seen the president for a week. Olney repeated the official version. "Cleveland was doing finely, was in good spirits and apparently enjoying excellent health," Olney told them. "His illness was all confined to his knee and foot."

The disinformation campaign worked. Most reporters who gathered near Gray Gables accepted the story that Cleveland did not have cancer and that he'd had no surgery, except the extraction of a rotten tooth. Some of them trusted Lamont's word. Others were swayed by Cleveland's truthful character. They couldn't imagine that he'd hide a cancer diagnosis and an operation.

'TWAS ONLY A BAD TOOTH

President Cleveland's Physician Says There Is No Cancerous Growth.

At This Time He Has Rheumatism in His Knee and Foot.

His Sister Has Been Sent for, but It is on Another and More Delicate Matter.

News of Cleveland's surgery leaked in July 1893. The White House denied the reports. From *Helena* [MT] *Independent*, July 8, 1893 (left), and *Daily Public Ledger* [Maysville, KY], July 7, 1893 (right).

CLEVELAND ILL

Confined to His Bed at Gray Gables With Rheumatism.

The Report That He Has Cancer Denied by His Physician.

VOL. 6. No. 154.

THE JUDGE.

ENTERED AT THE POST OFFICE AT NEW YORK AS SECOND CLASS MATTER. COPYRIGHT 1881 BY THE JUDGE PUBLISHING CO.

Price   NEW YORK, September 27, 1884.   10 Cents.

Another voice for Cleveland.

Cleveland had gained his honorable reputation by fighting corruption as mayor of Buffalo and governor of New York State. When he first ran for president in 1884, opponents in Buffalo accused then-bachelor Cleveland of fathering a child during a brief love affair ten years before. Newspaper articles gave the names of the mother and boy and accused Cleveland of refusing to take responsibility for his son.

When his allies asked Cleveland how they should respond to the accusation, he said, "Whatever you do, tell the truth." Even though he wasn't certain that he *was* the father, Cleveland declared that he was and that he financially supported the boy. The scandal didn't cost Cleveland the election. Instead, he earned respect from many voters for his honesty about an embarrassing incident.

Grover Cleveland was lying now, but his reputation protected him from exposure.

DON'T TELL THE VP

When Vice President Adlai Stevenson read the newspaper reports about the president's health, he set off from Chicago to Gray Gables to see whether they were true. Cleveland had been forced to put Stevenson on the ticket to get support for his presidential nomination within the split Democratic Party. He and Stevenson strongly disagreed about the way to handle the nation's economic situation.

Cleveland had to keep Stevenson away. If the vice president learned about the surgery, as he certainly would if he saw the president, he might use it

This cover of a weekly magazine, September 27, 1884, illustrates the political effect of Cleveland's admission that he'd fathered a baby out of wedlock. During his 1884 presidential campaign, his opponents used the phrase "I want my pa" to remind voters of Cleveland's behavior, considered immoral by many. He won the election anyway.

against Cleveland. By telegram, the president ordered Stevenson to visit the West Coast immediately and meet with Democratic leaders there. Travel in those days was restricted to trains, boats, and even stagecoaches. The western trip kept Stevenson out of the way for a month, allowing Cleveland time to heal in private.

Dr. Bryant remained at Gray Gables with the president during his recovery. Once the wound had healed sufficiently, Dr. Kasson Gibson was brought up from New York City. A specialized dentist, he could make an artificial jaw that would fill in the hole created by the removal of so much bone and tissue. Gibson worked in a small room at Gray Gables as he produced the rubber prosthesis. Once he positioned it inside Cleveland's mouth, the deformity in the president's face wasn't noticeable.

Grover Cleveland (right) and his 1892 running mate, Adlai Stevenson. Cleveland did not want Vice President Stevenson to find out about his 1893 cancer surgery.

By two weeks post-surgery, Cleveland looked and spoke as though nothing had happened. The rumors about his cancer and operation were fading away.

But just when Cleveland thought the episode was over, Dr. Bryant spotted some remaining diseased tissue on the edge of the wound. They'd have to operate again. Bryant reassembled the surgical team, except for Hasbrouck. No teeth would have to be removed this time.

Cleveland and Bryant boarded the *Oneida* at Gray Gables, announcing to reporters that they were going for a two-day fishing trip. Doctors Erdmann, Keen, Janeway, and O'Reilly had already been picked up at Elias Benedict's home in Greenwich, Connecticut. On July 17,

Cleveland and his wife, Frances, in 1893

the doctors performed a short surgery on the yacht to remove the worrisome tissue. Two days later, Cleveland returned to Gray Gables and his family. No one was the wiser.

The cover-up continued throughout July. Frances Cleveland repeated the false narrative on July 31 when she wrote a note to the Massachusetts governor thanking him for salmon he'd sent the family. She explained that Cleveland was taking a long restful vacation at Gray Gables after coping with the first several months of his presidency. "He came here completely worn out," she said, "and with an unusually bad attack of rheumatism besides."

Still, the secret surgeries weren't behind Cleveland yet.

SHOCKING DETAILS

E. J. Edwards was a journalist based in New York City who wrote a column for the *Philadelphia Press* under the pseudonym "Holland." In August, a doctor friend came to him with a juicy news scoop: President Cleveland definitely had a cancer operation during his mysterious absence in early July, just as some newspapers reported at the time. Edwards's friend heard all the details. He put Edwards in touch with an eyewitness to the surgery—the dentist Dr. Ferdinand Hasbrouck.

All along, Dr. Bryant suspected that Hasbrouck had been the source of the leak. In the aftermath of Cleveland's first operation, Bryant wouldn't let the medical team leave the yacht until he was sure the president had no complications requiring additional surgical care. This unexpected delay caused Hasbrouck to miss a planned procedure with another doctor in Greenwich. Because Bryant maintained tight secrecy, Hasbrouck couldn't notify this physician of the situation.

When Hasbrouck finally left the yacht a day late, his colleague was angry that the dentist hadn't shown up as scheduled. Hasbrouck explained what prevented him from coming. Such a momentous tale didn't stay secret for long. The news spread in the New York medical community. The rumor leaked to a few reporters in the days following the surgery, and vague articles about Cleveland's cancer appeared in newspapers. It also reached the ears of E. J. Edwards's friend.

After Edwards was tipped off, he set out to verify the story by visiting Hasbrouck in New York City. Edwards told the dentist everything he'd heard about the operation. Could Hasbrouck confirm it? The dentist assumed that one of the other eyewitness doctors had already revealed the truth. He said that the report was accurate, adding more information as the two men talked. Edwards never let on that Hasbrouck himself had been the source of the account.

On August 29, 1893, Edwards's column, "The President a Very Sick Man," appeared in the *Philadelphia Press* under his pen name, Holland. "It is useless longer to conceal the fact that Mr. Cleveland is a sick man, perhaps a very sick man," wrote Edwards.

The article confirmed the early-July press reports and added many details that Edwards collected from Hasbrouck. It recounted the "when" and "where" of the operation and how part of Cleveland's upper jaw had been removed. Edwards only provided part of the "who"—Bryant and Hasbrouck. He may not have known the other doctors' names. The column concluded by saying that nearly two months after the surgery, the physicians were cautiously optimistic that the cancer would not return and require another operation.

THE DENIALS

The Holland column was newsworthy since Edwards was the first journalist to have interviewed a person present at Cleveland's surgery. Newspapers nationwide republished it. The revelations shocked readers. A rumor even spread at the New York Stock Exchange that the president had died, creating alarm until someone confirmed that he was still alive.

Most newspapers expressed sympathy for Cleveland and the hope that his cancer wasn't deadly. Even those who had opposed his election wished him a full recovery, not the least because the country was experiencing an economic crisis. The *Indianapolis Journal* said, "It regarded his election as a national calamity, but it would regard his death in office as a greater one."

The *Seattle Post-Intelligencer* editorialized that Cleveland's death would lead to the disaster of Adlai Stevenson becoming president, a man the editors called "weak" and "frothy" and "vain." The newspaper added, "It is a serious reminder to the American people of the utter folly of selecting a cheap man for the second place on the national ticket."

NOW IT'S CANCER

Startling Statement Regarding Cleveland's Health.

The President Submits to An Oper-tion on the Yacht Onedia.

A Considerable Part of the Upper Jaw Bone Cut Away—He Was Kept in Bed Four Days, the Physicians Announc-ing the Disease as Rheumatism.

THE PRESIDENT A SICK MAN

An Operation Performed On Him Recently.

A PORTION OF HIS JAW REMOVED

Headlines from newspaper stories about E. J. Edwards's August 1893 article that exposed details of Cleveland's surgery. The White House used its influence with the press to stop the account from spreading. From the *Daily Public Ledger* [Maysville, KY], August 30, 1893 (left), and the *Delaware Gazette and State Journal* [Wilmington, DE], August 31, 1893 (bottom).

Those close to the president went into cover-up mode again. After reporters approached Dr. Hasbrouck about the Holland column, he repeated the original lie: Cleveland needed dental work. He told the *New-York Tribune*, "I saw nothing that would indicate disease of a cancerous nature." But he did tell the *Tribune* that W. W. Keen assisted Bryant with the surgery. Both Keen and Bryant denied Edwards's story.

When senators, representatives, and cabinet members in Washington were asked about the column, they claimed to know nothing about the surgery. And very few of them did.

The president's friend L. Clarke Davis, who edited the *Public Ledger*, spread the word that the Holland column was gossip created by Cleveland's enemies. The president had merely had a toothache requiring dental care. Some newspapers joined in to criticize Edwards, stating that no operation had ever been performed and calling his account a vicious personal attack and a lie—"a crime against decent journalism."

The day after the Holland article appeared, Cleveland traveled to Washington from Gray Gables. During the following weeks, he made several public appearances. People who saw him and heard him speak thought that he seemed perfectly healthy. They noticed no sign of a surgical scar. His voice sounded clear and strong. Surely, the Holland column had been wrong.

The campaign to smear Edwards worked.

Grover Cleveland privately acknowledged to some associates that there was truth in Edwards's column. In September, he wrote to his ambassador to Great Britain. Referring to the article, he attributed the reports to "a most astounding breach of professional duty on the part of a medical man. I tell you this in strict confidence, for the policy here has been to deny and discredit his story. I believe the American public and newspapers are not speculating further on the subject."

On September 1, Dr. Bryant wrote in his notes that the wounds in the president's mouth had healed. Cleveland would need the rubber prosthetic jaw permanently.

Grover Cleveland went on to finish his presidential term without more speculation about his surgery. He and his wife eventually had five children.

The second, Esther, was born on September 9, 1893, after her father recovered from his cancer operation. She is the only child of a president to be born in the White House.

After turning the presidency over to William McKinley in 1897, Cleveland retired to Princeton, New Jersey. He lived out his life there, rubbing shoulders with Princeton University's president, Woodrow Wilson, a future U.S. president who would have his own medical secrets. (See chapter four.)

During the next decade, Grover Cleveland's health declined. His mouth cancer never returned, but he was plagued with gastrointestinal and heart problems. On June 24, 1908, he died at age seventy-one after speaking his final words: "I have tried so hard to do right."

UNCOVERING THE COVER-UP

Although Grover Cleveland had gone to his grave, the tale of his cancer cover-up lived on. In September 1917, nearly a quarter century after his two surgeries on the *Oneida*, the whole truth was revealed, complete with never-before-told details.

Dr. W. W. Keen, who assisted with both operations on the *Oneida*, published his version of events after receiving permission from Cleveland's widow. His article appeared in the popular magazine the *Saturday Evening Post* rather than in a medical journal because Keen hoped to reach a larger audience. A few months later, he published a book version of his article.

In the book's foreword, Keen explained that Dr. Bryant intended to write about the surgeries himself after Cleveland's death. But Bryant died in 1914 without having done so. Except for Keen, Dr. Erdmann, and Elias Benedict (who owned the *Oneida*), everyone who had been part of the secret operations on the yacht had died. Keen wanted to set the record straight before all the eyewitnesses were gone.

He also was determined to clear the name of seventy-year-old journalist E. J. Edwards, whose reputation had been tarnished by Cleveland and his allies. Edwards's August 1893 account, wrote Keen, was almost entirely accurate.

After Keen's magazine article appeared, some people close to the cover-up spoke publicly. Among them was Robert O'Brien, editor of the *Boston Herald* and Cleveland's private secretary in 1893. "It was of the utmost importance that

Outgoing president, Grover Cleveland (right), stands beside his successor, William McKinley (center), as the new president is sworn in on March 4, 1897.

the affair should be kept secret," said O'Brien. "Few Americans ever knew how near the nation came to losing its President in the panicky summer of 1893."

THE FINAL DIAGNOSIS

After Cleveland's surgery, the dentist Kasson Gibson ended up with a sample of the president's diseased tissue. He saved it for years in a glass jar filled with liquid preservative. When Keen was working on his article, he asked Gibson to donate the specimens to the Museum of the College of Physicians of Philadelphia, a group with which Keen was associated. Gibson agreed, and the tumor in the glass jar was put on display at the college's Mütter Museum.

For decades, medical historians wondered whether the 1893 cancer diagnosis had been correct. Although oral cancers typically return, Cleveland never suffered a recurrence after his surgery. In 1976, a team of pathologists got permission from Cleveland's family and the museum to examine a piece of the sample.

They identified the tissue as verrucous carcinoma, a rare type of mouth cancer that usually doesn't spread to other parts of the body. Verrucous carcinoma wasn't identified until 1948, which explained why the pathologists in 1893 weren't sure about their diagnosis. Today the cancer is most commonly found in older men, especially those who use tobacco and drink alcohol. The usual treatment is to surgically remove it, just as Cleveland's doctors did.

Considering that the president's surgeons operated without modern instruments or antibiotics, the team did a remarkable job. Cleveland didn't bleed to death, he didn't develop an infection, he healed quickly. And he got away with a cover-up that lasted twenty-four years.

SURVIVED THE PRESIDENCY

Former President Grover Cleveland in 1908, shortly before he died in Princeton, New Jersey, at age seventy-one

WOODROW WILSON

28th **PRESIDENT**

BORN: December 28, 1856, in Staunton, Virginia

PROFESSION BEFORE PRESIDENCY: university professor of history and political science, president of Princeton University, governor of New Jersey

POLITICAL PARTY: Democrat

ELECTED: 1912 and 1916

SERVED: March 1913 to March 1921

DIED: February 3, 1924, in Washington, DC, age sixty-seven

PRESIDENTIAL TRIVIA:

★ Wilson was the only president to earn a doctoral degree. His was from Johns Hopkins University in political science.

★ He is the only president buried in Washington, DC (at the National Cathedral).

Thomas Woodrow Wilson in 1912, the year he was first elected president. (He dropped his first name during boyhood.)

CHAPTER FOUR
MISSING IN ACTION

"I seem to have gone to pieces."
—WOODROW WILSON

COLLAPSE

ON THURSDAY MORNING, OCTOBER 2, 1919, PRESIDENT WOODROW WILSON sat on the edge of his bed and tried to pick up a nearby water bottle. He couldn't move his left hand.

When his wife, Edith, entered the room, he told her he had no feeling in the hand. Could she help him to the bathroom? His left leg was numb and weak, but she managed to get him there.

Worried about his limp hand and trouble walking, she asked if he was all right for a few moments while she sent for the doctor. Using the private White House phone, Edith called the chief usher. "Please get Doctor Grayson, the President is very sick," she said.

Suddenly, she heard a sound from Wilson's room. Hurrying back to him, she discovered that he'd fallen off the toilet onto the bathroom floor. He was unconscious.

Edith grabbed a blanket and covered her husband so that he wouldn't catch a chill. By then, the president had regained consciousness.

Within a short time, White House physician Dr. Cary Grayson arrived. He and Edith lifted Wilson into bed. The left side of the president's body was paralyzed, including his leg, arm, and the lower part of his face.

Grayson contacted several other doctors to assist. Among the physicians were a Philadelphia nervous system specialist, the head of the Navy Medical School, and Edith's regular Washington doctor. The White House staff watched the arrival of the doctors and nurses throughout the day. They guessed that Wilson was ill, but no one told them anything.

Finally, late in the afternoon, Dr. Grayson called chief usher Ike Hoover into Wilson's room to help him rearrange furniture. Hoover was shocked when he saw the president on the bed. "He looked as if he were dead," Hoover recalled. "There was not a sign of life."

Woodrow Wilson had a long history of health problems before he entered the White House in 1913, some of which interfered with his education and work. These included headaches, indigestion, and frequent colds. At times, he suffered from more serious conditions.

In 1896, sixteen years before winning the presidency, Wilson experienced pain and numbness in his right hand. For many months, he couldn't use the hand to write, and he had to teach himself to use his left. Periodically, pain and numbness returned to his right hand and sometimes to his left shoulder and arm.

Wilson with his first wife, Ellen, and their three daughters at their summer home in Cornish, New Hampshire, in 1912, the year he was first elected president. Ellen was first lady for only seventeen months before she died at age fifty-four of Bright's disease, in August 1914. The same kidney ailment killed President Chester Arthur. (See chapter two.)

One morning in 1906, Wilson awoke blind in his left eye. A doctor diagnosed the cause as bleeding from a blood vessel in the eye. The physician told Wilson to rest and take a break from his intense work as Princeton University's president. Wilson's body gradually reabsorbed the blood, and his vision returned, though it wasn't completely normal again.

Historians and biographers disagree about the reasons for Wilson's health issues because few of his medical records remain. He was never hospitalized, and most of his doctors' notes were lost or destroyed.

Some historians claim that Wilson's numb right arm and temporary blindness were the result of strokes caused by hypertension (high blood pressure) and arteriosclerosis (thickened artery walls). They also attribute several physical crises after 1906 to strokes triggered by a blocked or narrow artery reducing blood flow to his brain.

Other historians argue that, instead of strokes, Wilson suffered from a nervous condition exacerbated by stress, causing occasional breakdowns. His arm and shoulder pain, they say, could have been the result of nerves and joints aggravated by his many hours of writing. His headaches and the damage to blood vessels in his eyes, brain, and elsewhere might have been signs of the early stages of hypertension and arteriosclerosis.

All agree on one thing, however: Based on the reported symptoms and the diagnosis by his doctors at the time, Woodrow Wilson suffered a devastating stroke on October 2, 1919. The left side of his body was paralyzed, and he was incapacitated both physically and—at least temporarily—mentally.

This was not what the public was told.

FIGHTING FOR THE LEAGUE

Wilson was fifty-six when he took the oath of office in March 1913 and came under the care of navy doctor Cary Grayson. Grayson had served on the presidential yacht during the administrations of Theodore Roosevelt (1901–1909) and William Taft (1909–1913). Wilson liked him and requested that Grayson be his White House physician.

Dr. Grayson recognized that Wilson had high blood pressure, digestive and nerve problems, and severe headaches. He encouraged the new president to eat a better diet and to get more exercise, sleep, and fresh air. In Wilson's day, no medications effectively treated high blood pressure, which eventually could lead to heart attack or stroke.

Wilson's health did improve. But he wasn't able to maintain this regimen once the demands of his job increased during the Great War (World War I). When the war broke out in Europe in July 1914, Wilson was reluctant to involve the United States. Most Americans wanted to stay out of the war, too. Then German submarines began to sink ships in the Atlantic Ocean, killing Americans.

In early April 1917, Wilson asked Congress to declare war on Germany, saying, "The world must be made safe for democracy." The United States entered the conflict, joining allies Great Britain, France,

WOODROW WILSON
President of the United States

"HE HAS KEPT US OUT OF WAR"

This is the face of a man strong, courageous, patient and kindly, a man---

Always alert to the aspirations of his fellow-man and sympathetic toward their fulfillment;

Never complacent toward the encroachments of privilege nor tolerant of social wrong;

Always seeking to enhance the dignity of labor and better the state of the toiler;

Never lending an ear to the sophistry of exploitation or the blandishments of expediency;

Always patient to hear and weigh, to appraise and analyze, and passionate to find the way of right;

Never premature in purpose nor prejudiced in judgment, and never headlong in decision—

Such is WOODROW WILSON.

A 1916 campaign ad from the *Monroe* [NC] *Journal*, October 27, 1916. Similar ads appeared in newspapers across the country, promoting Wilson's reelection. A campaign slogan was, "He has kept us out of war." Yet on April 2, 1917, just five months after winning a second term, President Wilson asked Congress to declare war on Germany. On April 6, the war resolution was passed, and America entered World War I.

Italy, and other countries. The fighting continued until November 11, 1918, when Germany agreed to a ceasefire.

In January 1919, Wilson led the American delegation at the Paris Peace Conference, during which the victorious Allies negotiated the terms of peace. Wilson's health suffered from the strain of negotiations over several months and from his four ship voyages across the Atlantic Ocean, each taking eight to ten days. He had bouts of colds, headaches, and digestive upsets.

While in Paris in early April, the president fell more seriously ill with coughing, diarrhea, vomiting, fever, and body aches. Dr. Grayson diagnosed the illness as a virus or influenza, the disease that killed millions worldwide during 1918–1919. Afterward, people around the president noticed a behavior change and said that "he was never the same after this little spell of sickness." Wilson became irritable and paranoid, and his memory seemed affected. Some historians think the president had a stroke, not the flu.

The Treaty of Versailles, the first of a series of peace treaties between the war's participants, was signed on June 28, 1919. Besides dealing with Germany, the agreement included the establishment of the League of Nations. Wilson had pushed hard for this international organization as a way to settle disputes and avoid another destructive world war.

In July, President Wilson brought the treaty home for the U.S. Senate to ratify, as required by the Constitution. He met with resistance from Republican senators who objected to parts of the treaty, particularly the League of Nations. They feared that the organization would again entangle

President Wilson and his White House physician, navy doctor Cary Grayson (left), returning to New York by ship from the Paris Peace Conference in early July 1919. Wilson crossed the Atlantic Ocean four times between December 1918 and July 1919, including a trip back to the U.S. in February and March 1919 to meet with Congress. Grayson always went along, attending the president from 1913 until Wilson's death. The doctor lived at the White House from 1913 to 1916 (when he married) and for several months after Wilson's October 1919 stroke.

This cartoon published July 10, 1919, shows President Wilson heading back to the White House after handing the peace treaty to the U.S Senate for ratification. Some Republican senators had already expressed concerns about the League of Nations.

the United States in the troubles of other countries and take away Congress's own power to declare war. After all the effort Wilson had put into negotiating the peace treaty, the entire agreement was in jeopardy of being rejected by the United States.

To gain the Senate's approval, Wilson believed he had no choice but to go directly to the public and urge them to pressure lawmakers to vote for the treaty. He planned a cross-country speaking tour at the end of the summer.

His wife and Dr. Grayson tried to dissuade him. They realized that he had been worn out by his European travels during the previous half year. He didn't seem completely recovered from his April illness in Paris either.

But Wilson had made up his mind. He told Grayson that he had a duty more important than his health. "The League of Nations is now in its crisis," he said, "and if it fails I hate to think what will happen to the world. . . . I must go."

On September 3, 1919, the speaking tour began. A train left Washington carrying President and Mrs. Wilson, Dr. Grayson, staff members, Secret Service agents, and dozens of reporters and photographers. The trip was grueling, filled with visits to cities, appearances before large crowds, and parades in the heat. Along the way, the train stopped so that Wilson could address small groups from the rear platform. He had always been a powerful orator, and he gave impassioned speeches that he had written himself about the importance of the league and the treaty.

Wilson used a train's rear platform for speeches during his 1919 cross-country tour. Here he addresses Illinois supporters from a train platform three years earlier, in January 1916. Dr. Cary Grayson stands on the left.

The tour soon began to wear on Wilson. He had constant headaches and wasn't able to sleep because of coughing spells and difficulty breathing. By the time the train headed back from the West Coast, Wilson was showing other signs of exhaustion. Dr. Grayson noticed that the left side of his face slightly drooped and that he drooled saliva from the left side of his mouth. On September 25, after stops in Denver and Pueblo, Colorado, the president had such an intense headache that he could barely see.

That night on the train, Wilson woke Edith to say his headache was excruciating. She sent for Grayson who found him nauseated and out of breath. The doctor was alarmed that Wilson "was on the verge of a complete breakdown." In his medical opinion, the tour must end and the train return to Washington immediately. Edith and Wilson's personal secretary, Joseph Tumulty, agreed.

The next morning, Grayson told the president of their decision. At first, Wilson objected. He desperately wanted to continue the trip. But he finally gave in. "I have never been in a condition like this," he admitted, "and I just feel as if I am going to pieces."

Grayson announced to the press that Wilson suffered from nervous exhaustion caused by the strain of the 8,000-mile speaking tour (about 12,900 km). It had affected his sleep and his digestive system. Wilson required a break from his presidential duties to rest.

THE COVER-UP

By the time Wilson returned to the White House on Sunday, September 28, he felt better. But the headaches continued.

Four days later, on Thursday morning, October 2, Wilson collapsed in his bathroom, paralyzed on his entire left side.

That day Grayson sent for other doctors to examine the president and give their opinion of his condition. Dr. Francis Dercum, a Philadelphia nervous system specialist, arrived at the White House late in the afternoon. Wilson was able to speak and follow directions during Dercum's exam, but he couldn't move his left arm or leg when instructed. Besides the paralysis, the doctor discovered that the vision in both eyes had been impaired. Dercum and Grayson decided that a stroke damaged the nerves on the left side of Wilson's body.

Edith strongly opposed revealing the diagnosis. Although all the consulting doctors wanted to make it public, they agreed to keep the secret out of respect for the family's wishes.

Dr. Grayson's bulletins to the press were general and never mentioned a stroke. At ten p.m. that evening, he released the statement: "The President is a very sick man. His condition is less favorable today and he has remained in bed throughout the day." Without identifying the cause as stroke, the bulletin added, "absolute rest is essential for some time." The White House told reporters that Wilson had to be protected from "worry and strain." No prediction was made about when he'd return to his presidential work.

Wilson married his second wife, Edith, on December 18, 1915. At forty-three, she was sixteen years younger than her husband. This photograph was taken the year of their marriage.

The cabinet members were in the dark about how sick Wilson was, and they couldn't get answers from the White House. Vice President Thomas Marshall was told nothing. Secretary of State Robert Lansing had been alarmed ever since Wilson returned early from his trip. The secretary of state was third in line to the presidency after the vice president. Lansing felt he had a responsibility to find out what was going on. Wilson was seemingly out of action, and someone had to make key decisions for the country.

On Friday morning, October 3, Lansing went to the White House and brought up the issue of presidential succession with Dr. Grayson and Joseph Tumulty. Lansing took out a book and read the succession clause of the Constitution: If the president was unable to carry out his duties, those powers should be taken over by the vice president. Lansing suggested that Vice President Marshall should be brought in to act in Wilson's place.

Tumulty was offended. "I have read the Constitution and do not find myself in need of any tutoring at your hands of the provision you have just read." He continued, "While Woodrow Wilson is lying in the White House on the broad of his back I will not be a party to ousting him." Dr. Grayson refused to say that Wilson was too disabled to perform his presidential duties.

Lansing failed to learn more about Wilson's condition. But over the weekend, the secretaries of the navy and agriculture managed to get Grayson and Tumulty to admit that the president was paralyzed on his left side. Both cabinet members were sworn to secrecy.

Secretary Lansing called a special meeting of the cabinet for Monday to discuss the crisis. At the meeting, he asked Dr. Grayson exactly what was wrong with the president and "was his mind clear or not." Grayson said it was and that Wilson "was very much annoyed when he found that the Cabinet had been called." That ended the cabinet's discussion about succession.

Vice President Marshall, who was turned away when he tried to see Wilson, wouldn't pursue taking over the presidential powers.

For more than a month, Wilson lay helpless in bed. The White House hid the extent of his incapacitation. He was shielded from visitors by his wife, doctors, and secretary. Medical bulletins to the press reported that he was gaining strength and making slow, steady progress. Grayson gave no specifics about Wilson's blood pressure, temperature, or pulse other than to say they were normal and that his mental processes were as good as ever.

When the doctor was questioned about whether Wilson had had a stroke, Grayson criticized those who made a diagnosis without seeing the patient.

By early December, members of Congress were increasingly concerned that Wilson's health was worse than the doctors had been letting on. Many believed that the nation should be informed of the facts. One senator told Secretary of State Lansing that "all this secrecy was having the effect of making people think that he must be wholly incapacitated and that someone was acting in his stead who had no legal right to do so."

Two senators—one Republican, one Democrat—asked to see Wilson to confirm that he was fit to act as president. The White House was forced to agree to the meeting. If anyone from Congress thought that the president was unable to function, it would rekindle talk of passing his duties to the vice president. Edith, Tumulty, and Grayson made certain that didn't happen.

When the senators arrived at the White House, they were taken to Wilson's sickroom where he lay in bed with his shoulders slightly propped up. His left hand and arm were covered by a blanket. The room was dimly lit. The senators were seated so that they couldn't get a good look at the left side of his face. Edith and Grayson stayed in the room to control the conversation if necessary.

The ploy worked, partly because one of the senators did most of the talking. Afterward, the two senators told waiting reporters that, though Wilson's voice didn't sound as clear as normal, his mind seemed alert.

THE ACTING PRESIDENT

For the next eighteen months, until Wilson's term ended, Edith Wilson took charge of the business that came to her husband's attention. She reviewed all letters and memos sent to him and decided which ones he would see. She wrote her own notes on documents and returned them to the sender.

Edith also screened who visited Wilson. If the vice president or cabinet members wanted to speak to him about a problem, she met them in her White House sitting room and relayed what she claimed the president wanted done. When Secretary of State Lansing asked for Wilson to act on several foreign matters, Edith refused to pass on the request. Early in 1920, two cabinet secretaries resigned. Edith offered the open positions to two new men, saying that they were Wilson's choices. Neither man had met with the president.

Edith maintained that she discussed all these presidential matters with her husband. The cabinet secretaries had doubts about who was making the decisions in the White House. They weren't sure whether Wilson's signature on documents was actually his or had been forged by Tumulty or Mrs. Wilson. Many in Washington believed that Edith was running things, even labeling her the first woman president or acting first man.

Dr. Grayson described her as standing "like a stone wall between the sickroom and the officials who insisted that their business was so important that they must see him."

Years later in her memoir, Edith stated that the doctors told her she had to shield Wilson from anything upsetting or stress-producing. Otherwise, her husband wouldn't recover. "Every time you take him a new anxiety or problem to excite him," she quoted Dr. Dercum as saying, "you are turning a knife in an open wound."

"How can I protect him from problems when the country looks to the President as the leader?" she asked him.

According to Edith, Dr. Dercum responded, "Have everything come to you; weigh the importance of each matter, and see if it is possible by consultations with the respective heads of the Departments to solve them without the guidance of your husband."

She claimed that when she suggested Wilson should resign, Dercum said that giving up the presidency would take away his will to recover. Saving her husband's life—that was Edith Wilson's justification for her actions from the day of his stroke until the end of his presidency.

For four months, Secretary of State Lansing continued to call cabinet meetings to keep the department secretaries working together and the executive branch operating. But in early February 1920, Lansing received a letter signed by the president asking him to resign. Wilson charged that Lansing had been disloyal and insubordinate by calling cabinet meetings when that right belonged only to the president.

The fact that Wilson had been told about the meetings all along made Lansing and others question the president's memory and mental state. Some wondered, too, if Wilson's displeasure with his secretary of state was related to Lansing's attempts to have the debilitated president's duties given to the vice president.

The *Los Angeles Times* called the president's decision "Wilson's Last Mad Act." The newspaper praised Lansing for keeping the executive departments functioning during Wilson's illness. "When the country saw the Cabinet continued to meet and the government departments were acting in unison[,] public confidence was restored." The newspaper said that axing Lansing would cost the Democrats the 1920 election.

Several days after Wilson requested Lansing's resignation, one of the doctors who had attended the president in October gave an interview to the *Baltimore Sun*. He let slip that Wilson had had a stroke. This was the first time anyone confirmed the rumored diagnosis. In response, the White House insisted that the president had never been incapacitated.

On February 28, 1920, the *Chicago Daily Tribune* criticized Dr. Grayson and Mrs. Wilson for preventing cabinet secretaries and foreign diplomats from meeting with the president. "This combination of the parlor and the sickroom has been the beginning and end of executive government, with a few exceptions." The newspaper went on to say, "The president thinks and acts with decision in some instances, but they are few. . . . No one has authority to act for the president, and some one in the succession to the presidency ought to have the authority."

Critics in the medical community and in Congress declared that, for the good of the country, Wilson's doctors and family should urge him to resign.

They had no intention of doing that.

DEFEATED

Although Wilson slowly began receiving a few visitors at the White House, he remained an invalid and made no public appearances. Meanwhile, Republican senators proposed changes to the Treaty of Versailles that would address their objections to the League of Nations. Many Democrats urged Wilson to agree to those changes to get the peace treaty ratified. The president refused to compromise. The Senate voted on the treaty twice— in November 1919 and March 1920—and it was defeated both times.

Wilson didn't attend a cabinet meeting until mid-April 1920, six months after his stroke. Before the cabinet secretaries were allowed into the meeting room, he was brought in by wheelchair and propped up in a chair at the table. Then, as each secretary entered, the man's name was announced. The secretary of treasury concluded that this was necessary because Wilson's memory or vision, or both, had been damaged by his stroke. Other cabinet secretaries later reported that the president couldn't follow the conversation and said little during the meeting. Edith and Dr. Grayson cut off the session by saying Wilson was tired.

At one point during the spring of 1920, Wilson mentioned to Grayson, "I have been thinking over this matter of resigning and letting

Wilson and his second wife, Edith, in the White House in June 1920. This is the first posed photograph taken after his October 1919 stroke. Designed to make the president look fully recovered, the photo doesn't show his paralyzed left side. Those who saw him in person said he had become "a shadow of his former self."

President Wilson (left) rides to the Capitol building with President-elect Warren Harding (1921–1923) on Inauguration Day, March 4, 1921. Because Wilson's physical condition left him unable to climb the stairs to the ceremony's outdoor site at the Capitol, he did not see his successor take the oath of office.

the Vice-President take my place. It is clear that I should do this if I have not the strength to fill the office." Wilson never brought up the subject again. In fact, he decided to run for a third term in the November 1920 election, convinced that he could get approval for the peace treaty and the League of Nations if he had more time.

Democratic leaders didn't let that happen. They knew that Wilson's stroke had weakened him physically and mentally. They worked behind the scenes to make sure he didn't have a chance to run again. In early July, delegates at the Democratic convention chose Ohio governor James Cox as their presidential nominee.

Wilson was certain that the American public would vote for the Democratic ticket to show their support for his foreign policy ideas. Instead, Republican Warren Harding, who opposed the League of Nations, won in a landslide. (See chapter five.)

Woodrow Wilson was awarded the 1919 Nobel Peace Prize as founder of the League of Nations. But the United States never joined the league, which weakened the group's influence on world affairs. The organization couldn't prevent World War II in 1939. In 1946, after the war ended, the league was replaced by the United Nations, of which the United States became a member.

Wilson wasn't the same after his stroke. His left arm and hand remained useless. He had to learn to walk again and always needed a cane for support of his left leg. When his term ended in March 1921, he

The retired President Wilson greets a crowd from the doorway of his Washington house on November 11, 1922—Armistice Day, which commemorated the end of fighting in World War I. Today in the United States, November 11 marks Veterans Day and honors all those who have served in the U.S. armed forces. Wilson was able to stand with a cane, but his left arm remained unusable after his 1919 stroke. The top of the cane is hooked in his coat pocket.

and Edith moved to a house in Washington, DC. They installed an elevator to accommodate his lameness. Steadily, his health deteriorated. He was nearly blind and had trouble concentrating.

"The machinery is worn out," he told Dr. Grayson one day. "I am ready." Not long after—on February 3, 1924—Woodrow Wilson died in his bed.

Grayson attributed his death to arteriosclerosis and the effects of the 1919 stroke that weakened his heart.

The day after his death, the *New York Times* ran a story detailing all the physical ailments which Wilson had kept secret. "Up to the time of his collapse [in October 1919] the country thought him a normally healthy man. But he was far from it." The article went on to say that Wilson ordered his stroke to be concealed from the public because it "might lead to a stock market panic, and possibly far-reaching consequences to a world then passing through the first stages of post-war reconstruction."

Lies were told. The president's condition was hidden. The transfer of duties to the vice president was thwarted. And Woodrow Wilson stayed in office.

In a photograph taken on December 12, 1923, less than two months before Wilson's death, his chauffeur-driven car stops during his daily ride so that he can buy Christmas Seals from a young girl. The sale of seals supported victims of tuberculosis. By this time, Wilson was nearly blind, unable to use his left hand, and couldn't walk without support.

WARREN HARDING

29th PRESIDENT

BORN: November 2, 1865, in Corsica (now Blooming Grove), Ohio

PROFESSION BEFORE PRESIDENCY: reporter, newspaper editor and owner, Ohio state senator and lieutenant governor, U.S. senator

POLITICAL PARTY: Republican

ELECTED: 1920, on his fifty-fifth birthday

SERVED: March 1921 to August 1923

DIED: August 2, 1923, in San Francisco, California, age fifty-seven

PRESIDENTIAL TRIVIA:

★ Harding was the first president elected after the Constitution's Nineteenth Amendment was ratified on August 18, 1920, giving women the right to vote.

★ Harding was the first president to have his voice broadcast over the radio, in May 1922.

Warren Gamaliel Harding in 1920, the year he was elected president

CHAPTER FIVE

THE DEADLY VOYAGE

"I am tired."
—WARREN HARDING

THE WHITE HOUSE PHYSICIAN

WARREN HARDING HADN'T BEEN PRESIDENT LONG WHEN HE REALIZED THE job might be too much for him. One day while he was swamped with letters to read and answer, he told a visitor, "I am not fit for this office and should never have been here."

He got there by winning a landslide victory in the November 1920 election against the Democratic Party's presidential nominee, Harding's fellow Ohioan James Cox. Cox's vice presidential running mate, Franklin Roosevelt, would become president himself a dozen years later. (See chapter six.)

The Republicans chose Harding as their candidate over several competitors. He was a U.S. senator, although not one who stood out for his accomplishments. Some said that the

Warren Harding's home on Mt. Vernon Avenue in Marion, Ohio, where he lived for thirty years. As a presidential candidate in 1920, Harding gave campaign speeches from the front porch to crowds in the street. By one count, as many as 600,000 people came to Marion to hear him. The cottage in the right, rear yard was the headquarters for national reporters who covered the campaign. A newspaperman himself, Harding visited there every day and made himself available for questions.

party leaders preferred him because he had shown that he would willingly go along with their plans and policies.

There was no denying that Harding looked like a president—handsome, distinguished, and nearly 6 feet (2 m) tall. He had a friendly personality, gave excellent speeches, and relished interacting with people. As a longtime newspaper owner and editor in Marion, Ohio, he knew how to use the press to his advantage. All of this helped Harding connect with the public.

Voters embraced his promise to return the country to "normalcy," which he described as the peaceful period before World War I and the influenza pandemic. Harding didn't support Woodrow Wilson's League of Nations, saying he didn't want the U.S. getting involved with other countries again as they had in the recent war. The majority of voters agreed. Harding and his running mate, Calvin Coolidge, coasted to victory.

When it was time for the Hardings to move into the White House in March 1921, Florence Harding insisted that her Marion doctor, Dr. Charles Sawyer, be brought along to care for her. She had long suffered from a painful kidney ailment that periodically debilitated her and had the potential to be fatal. Since Florence credited Sawyer with keeping her alive, Harding made him a brigadier general in the U.S. Army Medical Corps and the presidential doctor.

Warren Harding (left) and his vice president, Calvin Coolidge. To many voters, Harding looked presidential. He was almost 6 feet (2 m) tall and had a commanding presence.

Other military doctors in Washington weren't impressed by Sawyer. They considered him poorly trained, unaware of recent medical advances, and inclined to prescribe ineffective medications. A young naval medical officer, Dr. Joel Boone, was assigned to the presidential yacht to care for its crew and to the White House to care for the Hardings when Dr. Sawyer wasn't around. He observed Sawyer listening to a patient's heart by laying his ear on the chest instead of using a stethoscope. Boone was also concerned because Sawyer, who was in his sixties, had failing eyesight, which put him at a disadvantage when examining a patient and diagnosing illnesses.

Florence wasn't the only Harding with medical issues. When Warren was in his forties, his physician brother examined him and discovered that his blood pressure was too high. There were no cures or medications for this disorder then. Even though Harding looked and felt healthy, his brother advised rest and a better diet.

Warren dismissed it. Several relatives had died from cardiovascular ailments, and he thought his condition simply ran in the family. He told Dr. Sawyer, "I think that [the high blood pressure reading] is about normal for me, so I shall not give it any considerable worry."

Harding continued to maintain a busy schedule, overeat, smoke, and drink alcohol. By the time he became president at age fifty-five, his blood pressure was dangerously high. Although few doctors in the early 1900s grasped the connection, having high blood pressure, being overweight, and using tobacco and alcohol are all risk factors for heart disease and stroke.

THE GRIPPE

By his second year as president, Harding had noticeably aged. His hair was grayer, and he had less energy. He told a group of reporters, "I don't believe there is a human being who can do all the work there is to be done in the

President's office. It seems as though I had been President for twenty years." His blood pressure rose higher. Occasionally, he complained of chest pain. Dr. Sawyer diagnosed a digestive problem.

In late August 1922, Florence experienced an excruciating kidney attack that left her close to death. Dr. Sawyer kept the news away from the press until early September. Newspapers speculated that the first lady might not recover. Several nationally respected doctors were brought in to consult on the case. Before they and Sawyer could decide whether to fix the problem with surgery, Florence rallied, and her kidneys started working properly again. She later said she had willed herself to live. Her subsequent recovery was slow.

The stress of coping with his wife's illness took a further toll on President Harding. Dr. Boone

Warren and Florence Harding during his time as president. When they married in 1891, she was divorced with a young son. The couple never had children together. A skilled businesswoman, Florence helped Harding run his newspaper, the *Marion Star*.

observed that he seemed more fatigued than a year earlier. Sawyer wouldn't allow Boone to examine the president closely, insisting that Harding was *his* patient.

Then in January 1923, Harding developed a respiratory sickness that he couldn't shake. Dr. Sawyer told the press that it was the grippe, a term used for influenza. For several weeks, the president was too weak to get out of bed. At times he had indigestion and abdominal pain. His weakness and a persistent cough continued into the end of February. He was winded after the least exertion. As much as Harding wanted to work, he lacked the stamina to keep up his schedule.

Once Congress finished its session, Harding's presence in Washington was less important. He and Florence took a vacation to recuperate from their illnesses and the stress of his job. For five weeks in March and April, they traveled to warm Florida and Georgia where Harding could relax and play his favorite sport, golf.

But on the trip, the president had trouble catching his breath as he walked around the golf course. He often wasn't able to play all eighteen holes as he once had. When he returned to the White House after the vacation, press accounts said he looked rested and completely recovered from his illness. He wasn't.

Throughout the spring, Harding had chest pains that extended down his left arm—a symptom of heart problems. He was unable to lie flat in bed without gasping for breath. To sleep, he had to be propped up with pillows. It was a warning sign that the president's heart wasn't strong enough to efficiently pump blood from his lungs.

Dr. Sawyer told Dr. Boone and everyone else that both Hardings were doing very well. The president, however, shared with several close friends that he was exhausted and needed rest. He didn't get it.

THE VOYAGE OF UNDERSTANDING

With the presidential reelection campaign of 1924 on his mind, Harding and his advisors planned a 1923 summer-long trip across the United States. Harding hoped to increase his exposure to Americans and to find out more about them. He called the tour "The Voyage of Understanding." The trip included a visit to the Alaska territory, an area with many natural resources to develop that could benefit America's economy, including lumber, oil, coal, and minerals. No sitting president had ever been there.

Going with the president were about five dozen people including his wife, cabinet members, office staff, friends, reporters, and photographers. The group would travel across the continent by train to Tacoma, Washington, and then board the navy ship S.S. *Henderson* to Alaska. After a visit to California, the return journey to the White House at the end of August was to be by ship through the Panama Canal.

Dr. Sawyer and Dr. Boone both went along. As a naval doctor, Boone made medical arrangements for the sea travel. He was worried about Florence Harding's kidney problem and unsure that she could survive the long trip. He quietly arranged for a coffin to be loaded on the *Henderson* in case it was needed for her while they were at sea. Boone didn't realize that the president's health put him at greater risk than his wife.

Some of Warren Harding's friends advised him not to make the journey. They thought he was already too rundown. Dr. Sawyer, too, had concerns about the busy itinerary that called for Harding to make many public appearances and speeches along the way. This was not going to be a relaxing vacation. But Harding believed the trip was important.

On June 20, the presidential train left Washington, DC. As it made its way westward, it stopped in St. Louis, Missouri; Denver, Colorado;

Harding's Airedale terrier, Laddy, was a beloved celebrity. Here Laddy is photographed greeting his master at the White House in June 1922.

Salt Lake City, Utah; and Spokane, Washington. Other stops included smaller towns and two national parks—Yellowstone in Wyoming and Zion in Utah. Harding greeted crowds from the platform on the train's rear car during brief stops and spoke in large meeting halls on longer visits. Once the train reached the Pacific Ocean, the group traveled to Alaska by sea. Harding toured the territory for about two weeks.

THE FINAL STRETCH

Thursday, July 26

By the time the *Henderson* headed south from Alaska to its next stop in Vancouver, Canada, Harding was worn out from the intense schedule. He wasn't sleeping either.

In Vancouver, he tried to play golf, though he had trouble finishing the course. At one point, Dr. Boone, who was playing with him, asked, "How are things going, Mr. President?"

"Not at all well, Boone," Harding replied. "I don't feel too well."

Later in the day, Boone informed Dr. Sawyer that Harding was ill.

That evening, the *Henderson* sailed for Seattle, Washington, where the group planned to board the train again. During the night, the president had upper abdominal pain and felt nauseated. Dr. Sawyer gave him medicine to treat his discomfort. No record exists of what the medication was.

Sawyer blamed the illness on spoiled crabmeat that Harding ate in Vancouver. He told reporters that others in the entourage had been ill, too. Boone knew that wasn't true.

Friday, July 27

The *Henderson* arrived in Seattle in early afternoon. Florence, Sawyer, and Boone all advised Harding to skip the day's plans because he'd been sick the night before. Harding resisted. People had come to see him, and he was going to show up. "Of course, we are going to go ashore!"

On that sunny afternoon, Harding rode in a parade car and made several public appearances. Dr. Boone watched him carefully, growing more worried about signs of fatigue. In late afternoon, Harding gave a lengthy speech to a stadium full of enthusiastic spectators at the University of Washington. It did not go well.

As the speech continued, he sounded out of breath and slurred his words. He mistakenly said "Nebraska" instead of "Alaska." At one point, Harding dropped the pages of his speech, and Secretary of Commerce Herbert Hoover had to pick them up and reorder them for him. Although no one knew then what was happening, Harding's heart was unable to pump enough oxygenated blood to his brain when he stood for a long period.

On the train that night, the president tried to sleep while it headed to California's Yosemite National Park. But he experienced severe abdominal cramps again, even worse than the night before. Florence stayed up with him.

Saturday, July 28

In the morning, the ailing Harding cancelled the Yosemite visit. The train diverted to San Francisco so that he could rest for a few days before resuming his California schedule.

Dr. Sawyer announced to the press that Harding had been sick on Thursday night. The illness worsened Friday night, giving the president pain. Sawyer repeated that Harding had a slight case of ptomaine poisoning from spoiled crabmeat. What he needed most was rest.

Various spokesmen traveling with the president downplayed his ailment as temporary and minor. Dr. Hubert Work, Harding's new secretary of the interior and a physician, told reporters that they were sure the president would "promptly be restored to his normal condition of splendid health."

In fact, Warren Harding hadn't been in splendid health for several years.

Behind the scenes, Sawyer and Boone agreed that both Hardings were in jeopardy. They convinced Florence that she needed to get some sleep while the train traveled to San Francisco. She agreed as long as Boone stayed by Harding's side.

The doctors discussed their concerns with the cabinet officers aboard the train. In reaction, Secretary Hoover sent a telegram to a good friend of both his and Work's—Dr. Ray Wilbur, the president of Stanford University and a well-known physician. Hoover asked Wilbur to meet them in San Francisco the next day (Sunday) and to bring one of Stanford's best doctors with him.

That night the president had difficulty breathing. During a short stop when there was a break from loud train noises, Harding awoke. Boone took the opportunity to check him over. When the doctor tapped the president's chest and listened to his heartbeat, he knew something was wrong. He doubted that Harding had food poisoning, as Dr. Sawyer told the press. Boone's examination revealed that the president's heart was enlarged— a sign that the heart muscle had weakened and couldn't effectively pump blood through his body.

Sunday, July 29

The train pulled into San Francisco about eight in the morning. The doctors planned to take Harding off the train by stretcher. The president rebelled against that. "I will not be carried off this train!" he said firmly. He wasn't going to meet the state and city dignitaries in his pajamas nor let the public see him as a sick man.

Harding dressed, complete with his hat. After greeting the governor and mayor, he and Florence walked from the train to a waiting limousine. When the limo reached the Palace Hotel, the president walked through the lobby to the elevator. On the eighth floor, he continued down the hall to the Presidential Suite. Then he collapsed across the bed in utter exhaustion.

Late that night, Stanford's Dr. Ray Wilbur came to the hotel with Dr. Charles Cooper, an expert on heart and lung diseases. When the two physicians examined Harding, they noted that his blood pressure was elevated, his heart was beating rapidly, and the area around the gallbladder was tender. Like Boone, they diagnosed an enlarged heart.

At 11 p.m., the president's assistant released a statement saying that Harding was ill and regrettably had to cancel his entire California itinerary. Again, Dr. Sawyer told the press that the president needed rest after his ptomaine poisoning.

Monday, July 30

At nine in the morning, the doctors—Sawyer, Boone, Work, Wilbur, and Cooper—convened to discuss the president's condition with him and his wife. Florence vetoed taking the president to the hospital. After all, he had five doctors and two nurses to care for him at the hotel. If Harding went to the hospital, the country might panic.

The five doctors issued a bulletin to the press sharing the president's elevated temperature, pulse, and breathing rate. The report stated that Harding suffered from a gallbladder attack. Because he'd kept up his busy schedule while he was ill, he'd "temporarily overstrained his cardiovascular system."

For the next several days, the doctors released updates two or three times a day to the four dozen or so reporters who were set up in the hotel.

Dr. Boone later admitted that Sawyer, who was always more optimistic than the other doctors, influenced the tone of the bulletins.

When Sawyer talked to the press, he continued to say that food poisoning was at the root of the president's health problems and that it had affected his gallbladder. According to Sawyer, Harding's body was so run down that he couldn't fight the poisons from the ptomaine attack. But in the medical bulletins, the other doctors described Harding's symptoms in a way that they knew physicians everywhere would recognize as signs of a heart condition.

Later Monday, an X-ray machine was brought from a hospital to check Harding's lungs for pneumonia. The evening bulletin mentioned a cough. The chest X-ray showed pneumonia in the president's right lung. "His condition is grave," the doctors' report said.

For the first time, the public learned that the president's illness was serious.

Tuesday, July 31

Harding had trouble sleeping, and the doctors gave him the drugs digitalis and caffeine to help his heart function better. This allowed the president to get a decent night's rest. According to the Tuesday morning bulletin, he now felt less tired. He was still running a temperature but continued to improve.

The news of his illness generated criticisms, however. The *New York Times* on July 31 questioned whether Harding should have made the trip in the first place. Ever since Woodrow Wilson suffered a stroke on his western tour, the article said, many believe "that Presidents owe it to the country not to take such long journeys."

The newspaper also brought up the Constitution's vague meaning about a president's "Inability to discharge the Powers and Duties" of the office.

President Harding welcoming children at the White House during his presidency

Who should decide that the president is disabled? Who should take over during that period?

Before his trip, Harding left Secretary of State Charles Evans Hughes in charge of calling cabinet meetings if necessary. The *Times* pointed out that, according to the Constitution, it was "the duty of the Vice President to act for the President," not the secretary of state.

Wednesday, August 1

When the doctors checked Harding's lungs, they were pleased that the pneumonia was slowly clearing up. The president was able to eat a bit, and his temperature was normal. The Wednesday medical bulletins made no specific mention of his enlarged heart.

Dr. Sawyer remarked to a reporter, "I think I may say that he is out of danger, barring complications."

But in Boone's opinion, Harding "was not doing as well as we would have liked." Even the president told his doctors that he was worried about his heart.

Thursday, August 2

As morning dawned in the San Francisco hotel, Harding still felt worn out, and his breathing rate was twice what was considered normal. But his lungs were much better. "It looks as though we are out of the woods now," Harding commented to Dr. Work.

Newspaper articles that day said that Harding's pneumonia was under control and his breathing was returning to normal. The *New York Times* reported that, although the president hadn't fully mended, "there is every indication that he ultimately will recover health and strength." The public was relieved at the news.

The doctors' morning bulletin announced, "We are more confident than heretofore as to the outcome of his illness." The afternoon bulletin was positive, too. "The President has had the most satisfactory day since his illness began," it said.

THE END

Before going to dinner on Thursday evening, Dr. Boone looked in on the president. While Harding rested, Florence was reading to him. Dr. Sawyer and one of the nurses were there, too.

Then without warning, Harding became pale and broke out in a soaking sweat. As the two doctors rushed to his aid, he said he felt quite strange.

After the nurse changed him into dry pajamas, Harding commented, "Now I feel perfectly comfortable." His pulse had slowed, and his color returned. He asked his wife to keep reading.

Confident that the crisis was over, Boone left for dinner, and Sawyer stepped out of the room for a moment.

Not long after, Harding remarked that he liked what Florence read. "That's good. Go on," he said.

Those were the president's last words. He seemed to shudder slightly. And then he slumped over.

Florence called out for help. The doctors were alerted and hurried to the room. There was nothing they could do. Warren Harding was gone. The time of death was officially recorded as 7:20 p.m.

The end was a shock. Dr. Wilbur recalled, "It took nearly an hour before I could finally convince Mrs. Harding that the President was dead."

The reporters in the hotel learned about Harding's death almost immediately and spread the word across the country. Around midnight, the

HARDING'S DEATH STUNS NATION; PRESIDENT COOLIDGE SWORN IN

PRESIDENT HARDING DIES FROM APOPLEXY; END COMES INSTANTLY AS WIFE IS READING TO HIM; HAD SEEMED NEARING RECOVERY

After reading that President Harding was recovering, the public was shocked to see headlines like these on the morning of August 3, 1923, from the *Washington Post* (top) and the *Los Angeles Times* (bottom).

doctors released their bulletin. It recounted Harding's illness during the previous week and mentioned his medical history of high blood pressure, chest pain, enlarged heart, and likely thickened artery walls (arteriosclerosis). This was information about the president's health that had never been made public by him or Dr. Sawyer.

The bulletin discussed Harding's recent gastrointestinal upset that caused pain in his abdomen and a fever. The doctors believed he'd had a gallbladder attack. The bulletin did not mention food poisoning.

It concluded by saying Harding "died instantaneously without a word or a groan" while he was recovering from a temporary illness. The cause of death was the bursting of a blood vessel in the brain—a stroke—that could have happened "at any time."

President Harding's death stunned the nation. The medical updates in the newspapers made people think he was getting better. Few knew how seriously ill Harding was. Few were aware that he'd had symptoms of heart disease for years.

The news was a surprise to the vice president, too. Calvin Coolidge was told that Harding was ailing, but as he wrote in his autobiography, "The official reports which I received from his bedside soon became so reassuring that I believed all danger past." Shortly before midnight Eastern Time on August 2, about an hour and a half after Harding died, Coolidge received the message that he was now the president.

THE SCANDALS

When he died, Harding was a popular president. An estimated three million people came to see his funeral train make its way from San Francisco back to Washington and—after services in the U.S. Capitol—on its final trip to Marion, Ohio.

Harding was known for assembling a cabinet of several impressive men who later became significant leaders. Two went on to be president (Vice President Calvin Coolidge [1923–1929] and Secretary of Commerce Herbert Hoover [1929–1933]), and one served as the chief justice of the Supreme Court (Secretary of State Charles Evans Hughes).

But within just a few months of Harding's death, it became clear that not

The Harding Memorial Presidential Gravesite was built in Marion, Ohio, with private funds and dedicated in 1931. Harding wanted to be buried near a tree under the sky. He and Florence (who died in 1924) are interred in the roofless center of the memorial next to a small tree.

all his appointees had been good choices. His attorney general, his interior secretary before Dr. Work, and his head of the Veterans' Bureau were separately tried for accepting payoffs and engaging in corrupt schemes. Harding wasn't accused of directly benefiting from these deals. Still, many Americans thought he should have been less trusting of his friends.

Harding's reputation was further damaged by scandals involving his personal life that surfaced after both he and his wife had died. Throughout his marriage, there were whispered stories about Harding's extramarital affairs. In 1927, a woman who grew up in Marion and was thirty years younger than Harding wrote a sensational book. Nan Britton claimed that while he was a senator, Harding fathered her daughter, Elizabeth, born in 1919. Britton said he regularly paid for their child's care although he never saw the girl. Britton was angry that Harding hadn't provided for them in his will. Her book was a bestseller.

While Britton's story rang true for some people in Marion and Washington and for many in the public, others thought she was lying. The controversy wasn't settled until 2015, based on genetic testing unavailable in the 1920s. Elizabeth died in 2005, but DNA from the families of Harding and Elizabeth proved that Warren Harding was, indeed, her father.

Soon after Harding's death, his wife burned letters and documents from his offices and desks in Marion and Washington. Many suspect that Florence was aware of at least some of the scandals and was trying to destroy evidence incriminating her husband. Part of that paper trail escaped her fires, however.

In 1963, a Harding biographer uncovered love letters from the president to a female family friend in Marion. The letters, kept by her and long hidden, revealed that their affair had gone on for fifteen years, ending in 1920. The letters are now at the Library of Congress and accessible online.

CONSPIRACY THEORIES

Harding's death certificate attributed his death to a stroke. But Dr. Wilbur, who signed it, later wrote that no one would ever know for certain what caused the president to die. Florence Harding had refused to allow an autopsy of her husband.

The lack of an autopsy was exploited in 1930 when a convicted con artist claimed in a book, *The Strange Death of President Harding*, that the president had been murdered. The author charged that Florence poisoned Harding with help from Dr. Sawyer, because she was jealous of her husband's young mistress and their child. That was why she prevented an autopsy. Both Florence and Sawyer died in 1924 and couldn't challenge the story.

As with most hoaxes and disinformation, this account contained enough elements of truth to convince many readers. Dr. Sawyer had repeatedly told the press that the president had ptomaine poisoning from spoiled crabs. And at the time the book came out, Nan Britton had recently accused Harding of fathering her daughter. Three years later, the poisoning tale in the con artist's book was exposed as a fabrication. Harding had not been poisoned.

Knowledge of heart disease and its symptoms has progressed in a hundred years. Modern medical experts agree: Harding's final moments fit a heart attack, not a stroke. The seizure he had shortly before his death is typical when the heart nearly stops beating. The body reacts with a burst of adrenaline which causes perspiration. His fatal heart attack came soon after. Some historians think that Harding's symptoms in January and February, seven months before his death, indicated that he'd had a heart attack then, too.

Dr. Sawyer treated Harding for years, but apparently he failed to recognize his patient's life-threatening heart disease.

Harding's death certificate, signed by Dr. Ray Lyman Wilbur of Stanford University, states that at 7:20 p.m., August 2, the president died of a stroke (cerebral apoplexy) following an acute gastrointestinal infection, including an inflamed gallbladder (cholecystitis), and pneumonia. According to the certificate, Harding's thickened blood vessels (arterial sclerosis) over several years contributed to his death. Food poisoning was not mentioned.

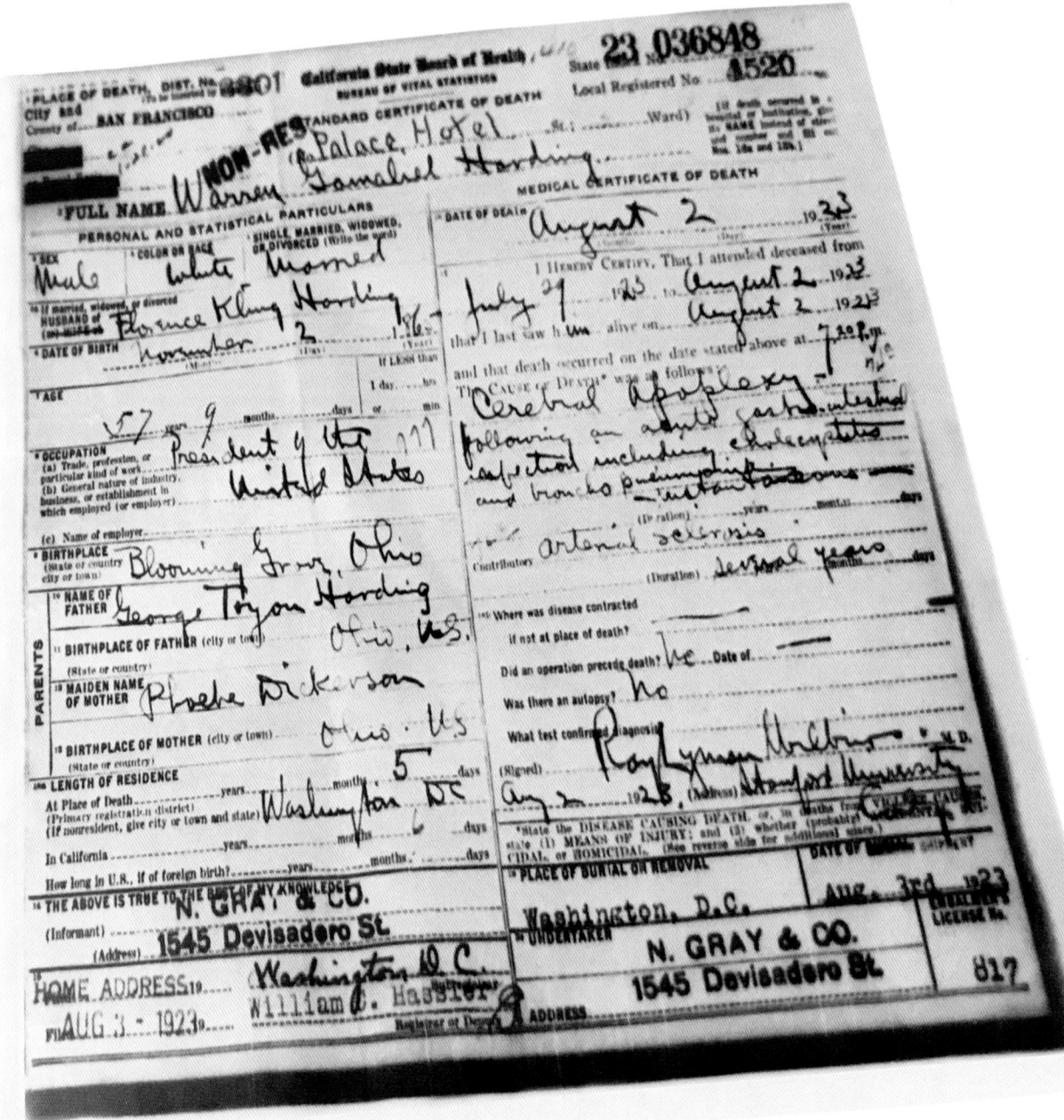

During the century after Harding's death, many historians considered him one of the worst presidents, partly because of his administration's corruption. Other historians argue that Harding deserves more recognition for his accomplishments. They credit him with pushing Congress to set up a Bureau of the Budget to make government spending efficient. They also believe that during his short time in office, the economy—weakened by World War I—became more prosperous.

One fact is not in dispute. As Dr. Ray Wilbur recalled: "Harding came to San Francisco a very sick man." He left the city in a coffin.

FRANKLIN ROOSEVELT

32nd PRESIDENT

BORN: January 30, 1882, in Hyde Park, New York

PROFESSION BEFORE PRESIDENCY: lawyer, New York state senator, assistant secretary of the U.S. Navy, governor of New York

POLITICAL PARTY: Democrat

ELECTED: 1932, 1936, 1940, and 1944

SERVED: March 1933 to April 1945

DIED: April 12, 1945, in Warm Springs, Georgia, age sixty-three

PRESIDENTIAL TRIVIA:

★ In 1937, Roosevelt became the first president to be inaugurated on January 20. The Twentieth Amendment, adopted in 1933, changed Inauguration Day from March 4.

★ Roosevelt was the only president to be elected four times. He served twelve years, longer than any other president. The Twenty-Second Amendment, adopted in 1951, limited presidential terms to no more than ten years (two elected four-year terms and up to two years of another president's term).

Franklin Delano Roosevelt in 1936, the second time he ran for president

CHAPTER SIX

AN IMAGE MANIPULATED

"Repetition does not transform a lie into a truth."
—FRANKLIN ROOSEVELT

TRUE OR FALSE?

IN THE FALL OF 1939, THE WORLD WAS ON EDGE. ON SEPTEMBER 1, GERMAN dictator Adolf Hitler ordered an invasion of Poland. Two days later, the United Kingdom and France, in support of Poland, declared war on Germany. World War II in Europe had begun. During the next six years, the fighting would devastate countries and result in the deaths of tens of millions of their citizens.

From the beginning of the conflict, many people in the United States cautioned against getting involved. They hadn't forgotten the deaths of their young men twenty years before in World War I. At the end of October 1939, President Franklin Roosevelt gave a radio speech to reassure the country. He dismissed the multiple reports which claimed that he

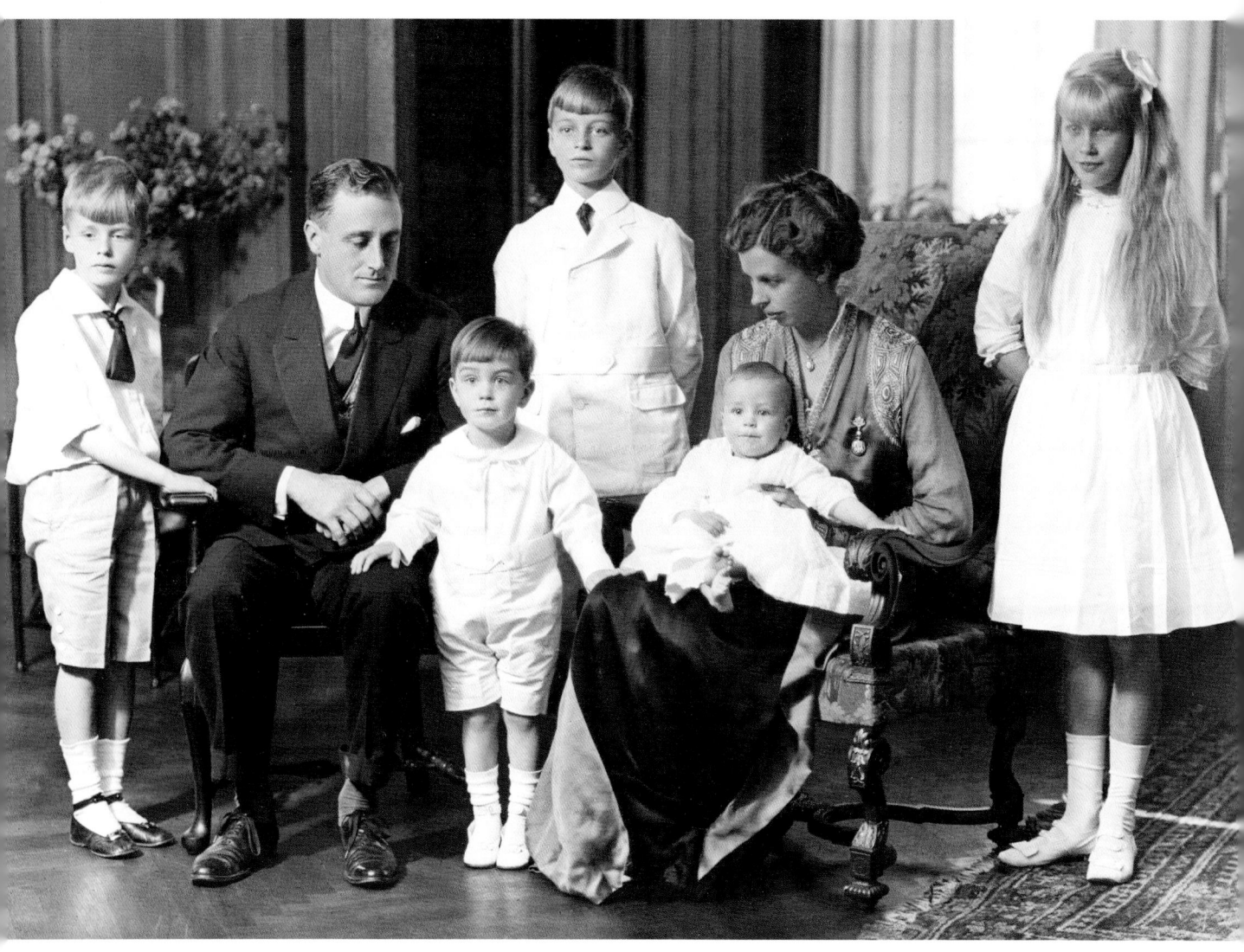

Franklin Roosevelt with his wife, Eleanor, and their five children, in 1916. Eleanor's uncle, Theodore Roosevelt, the twenty-sixth president, gave her away at her wedding.

planned to send soldiers to Europe again. Roosevelt called those propaganda and rumors. "The United States of America, as I have said before, is neutral and does not intend to get involved in war." He ended his speech with the line, "Repetition does not transform a lie into a truth."

Yet Roosevelt, his aides, and his doctor repeatedly lied about his health. They shut down questions about his fitness to govern. They directed which photographs of him could be published. Throughout the longest presidency in American history, Roosevelt and his associates intentionally hid the truth.

A DISTRESSING DIAGNOSIS

Franklin Roosevelt was born into a wealthy family and grew up on an estate in Hyde Park, New York, north of New York City. After receiving his early education from private tutors and a boarding school, he graduated from Harvard University in the class of 1904. The next year, he married his distant cousin Eleanor Roosevelt, who was the niece of former President Theodore Roosevelt, a man Franklin idolized. The couple had six children, one of whom died as an infant.

Roosevelt trained to be a lawyer at Columbia Law School and began practicing in New York City. His real ambition, however, was to go into politics as his cousin Theodore had. In 1910, when he was twenty-eight years old, Roosevelt won a seat in the New York State Senate as a Democrat. His political career took off after he supported Woodrow Wilson in the 1912 presidential campaign. The victorious Wilson rewarded Roosevelt by appointing him assistant secretary of the navy, a post he held throughout World War I.

Tall and handsome with an outgoing personality, Roosevelt made an impression on leaders in the Democratic Party. In 1920, they nominated him to be the vice presidential candidate on the ticket with presidential

Roosevelt campaigns as the Democrats' 1920 vice presidential candidate. Republican Warren Harding won the election in a landslide and became the next president.

nominee James Cox. After the pair lost to Warren Harding and Calvin Coolidge, Roosevelt resumed his career in New York City as a lawyer and the vice president of a financial firm.

In August 1921, he went on vacation with his family to their summer home in Campobello, New Brunswick, Canada. One afternoon, he fell ill with a chill and achy muscles. In the morning, Roosevelt had a high fever and pain in his limbs. The symptoms steadily worsened.

Eventually, he was diagnosed with poliomyelitis, or polio, a dreaded disease that typically strikes children and is sometimes fatal. The polio virus can affect the nervous system and cause paralysis. It usually spreads from an infected person's feces into the mouth of the victim, often through contaminated water. In 1921, doctors didn't understand much about the disease. There was no effective treatment or preventative.

From the beginning, Roosevelt's family controlled the news about his illness. A *New York Times* article on September 16, 1921, reported that Roosevelt was sick with poliomyelitis and had lost use of both legs. But his doctor told the newspaper, "You can say definitely that he will not be crippled. No one need have any fear of permanent injury from this attack."

This statement proved incorrect. Many patients did fully recover from a polio attack. Yet despite months of care and intense effort on his part, Franklin Roosevelt's legs were permanently paralyzed from the hips down. He had always been active and enjoyed swimming, hiking, skating, and dancing. Now he had to depend on others to get through a day.

Roosevelt wasn't able to support his weight without steel braces on his legs. To stand alone, he had to hold on to or lean against a solid object, such as a railing or post. To move forward, he used crutches to swing his legs along.

He perfected the appearance of walking without crutches by holding the arm of an aide (frequently one of his sons), who essentially carried him along while he balanced himself on his other side with a cane. Using upper torso muscles that he strengthened through exercise, Roosevelt moved his body back and forth and propelled himself forward. The effort was physically demanding, but he kept a broad smile on his face to hide his struggle from observers.

In 1924, Roosevelt traveled to Warm Springs, Georgia, where the buoyancy of the warm mineral-rich water allowed him to move his legs in a way he couldn't on land. Because he visited often, Roosevelt built a cottage there. Using his own money, he set up a clinic at Warm Springs to help other polio victims. He also started an organization to raise funds for polio research, later called the March of Dimes Foundation.

Roosevelt sits by the swimming pool in Warm Springs, Georgia, in 1924. The photograph shows his thin legs. After his polio attack, his leg muscles would never again support him despite his attempts to strengthen them through exercise. He built up the muscles in his upper body to steady himself when taking steps using crutches or leaning on another person.

By the early 1950s, this investment paid off when a vaccine to prevent polio was developed.

Some people close to Roosevelt believed that coping with polio made him more compassionate, patient, and able to deal with difficulties. He later said, "If you had spent two years in bed trying to wiggle your big toe, after that anything else would seem easy!"

PATH TO THE WHITE HOUSE

Roosevelt returned to politics in 1928 when the Democratic Party asked him to run for New York governor. He agreed. He had presidential aspirations and didn't want to lose the goodwill of the party's leaders.

His health became an issue in the campaign. His opponent exploited voters' concerns about whether a paralyzed man would be able to perform the work required of a governor. Roosevelt dealt with the problem by trying to hide his disability. He led voters to think that he was cured of polio and back to normal. His aides convinced photographers not to snap pictures of him sitting in a wheelchair or being lifted from a car.

To show that he was energetic and vigorous, Roosevelt traveled all over New York by car and train. He gave speeches perched on a car's backseat or standing with his braces covered by his pant legs. Although the Democrats' national presidential ticket lost to Republican Herbert Hoover, Roosevelt won the governorship.

A year later, the prosperous 1920s ended with the 1929 stock market crash. An economic depression followed. Factories and businesses closed, millions of workers lost their jobs, prices for farmers' crops fell, and banks failed. People who owed money lost everything when their debts were called in and they couldn't pay. As the Great Depression continued, the public became frustrated that President Hoover wasn't doing more to solve their economic woes. An opportunity opened for Franklin Roosevelt.

At the Democratic Party's 1932 nominating convention, the delegates chose Roosevelt as their presidential candidate to challenge Hoover. Roosevelt's opponents used his disability to argue against his election. They claimed that voters deserved a powerful leader who would rescue them from the Depression, not someone physically incapacitated.

Once again, Roosevelt and his aides hid the extent of his paralysis, attacking anyone who brought it up. The Democratic national chairman, James Farley, criticized those who insinuated that Roosevelt was unfit to serve. His lameness didn't affect his overall health, said Farley, anymore "than if he had a glass eye or were prematurely bald."

Going further, the Roosevelt team arranged for their allies to put out the word that he had overcome polio and would walk again soon. The health commissioner of Buffalo, New York, (Roosevelt's physician friend) stated that the candidate's condition was a "temporary, partial disability of some of the leg muscles."

In fact, the disability of his legs was neither temporary nor partial, and Roosevelt knew it. Most voters did not.

During the campaign, Roosevelt was careful to conceal his braces, wearing pants cut longer so that the metal didn't show when he sat down. He never allowed himself to be spotted using crutches. Whenever he stood to give a speech at a lectern, aides carefully blocked the view after he finished. That prevented anyone from seeing him awkwardly let go of the lectern and grab his crutches.

Roosevelt promised to give Americans a "New Deal" that would end the Depression. The voters liked what he said, and in the November election, he won a huge victory over Hoover. Roosevelt had reached his goal of becoming president of the United States.

Roosevelt (middle) at his first presidential inauguration, March 4, 1933. He uses a cane and holds on to his son James's arm. With this support and braces on his legs, Roosevelt appeared to walk.

SHAPING THE IMAGE

Shortly after his inauguration, the new president chose his White House physician. By tradition, the president's doctor was an active duty military officer. These physicians were already paid by the government, and they could be trusted to be discreet about anything they saw or heard.

From his days as navy assistant secretary, Roosevelt knew President Wilson's doctor, Cary Grayson. When he asked for a recommendation, Grayson named Dr. Ross McIntire at the Naval Hospital. McIntire's expertise was the eyes, ears, nose, and throat. Grayson thought he would be an ideal match for Roosevelt, who often suffered with sinus trouble.

Dr. McIntire and Roosevelt's aides made sure the country saw the president as robust and active. The press was told that he swam and exercised in the White House pool every day and that his only reported medical problems were colds. The White House discouraged reporters from referring to his disability. For the most part, they cooperated and didn't mention Roosevelt's paralysis or his use of a wheelchair.

His team carefully choreographed public events to hide his condition. They cautioned photographers to take images of the president only from the waist up. If Secret Service agents noticed a photographer aiming at the president in his wheelchair, they grabbed the camera and destroyed the film. Photographers were afraid that they'd lose their White House access if they took revealing pictures. Less than a handful of photographs of Roosevelt in a wheelchair were published during his political career.

Many Americans never realized that their president couldn't stand or walk without help. They assumed he had regained use of his legs after his polio illness, which was exactly what the White House wanted them to think.

With his friendly manner, the president courted the Washington-based reporters. He gave frequent press conferences in the Oval Office during which he always provided the journalists with newsworthy information. In this way, Roosevelt gained their favor and influenced the articles they wrote about him. After Roosevelt had been president a year, an item appeared in the *New York Herald Tribune* titled "The President's Good Health." It gushed that "he is bearing the terrible strain of the Presidency without fatigue. . . . May the President's health and happiness know no halt!"

By the end of Roosevelt's first term, however, some editorial pages had become critical of his New Deal programs and government spending. They warned that Roosevelt was leading the nation toward socialism. Instead of pulling the country out of the Depression, they charged, the economy had slipped further behind.

Roosevelt went directly to the voters. To mold public opinion on various subjects without depending on newspaper editorials, he used

In July 1937, President Roosevelt holds a microphone as he prepares to address a church group in Mount Marion, New York. By sitting in the car, he was able to hide his disability.

his radio-broadcasted fireside chats, which started soon after his March 1933 inauguration.

Roosevelt ran for reelection in 1936 and won in a landslide. In 1940, he decided to run for a third term, something no previous president had done. He won again.

WAR

Despite President Roosevelt's October 1939 statement about keeping the U.S. out of World War II, everything changed on December 7, 1941. That Sunday, Japan attacked Pearl Harbor, Hawaii. Dozens of U.S. military ships and planes were destroyed and roughly 2,400 service members were killed. Roosevelt called it "a date which will live in infamy."

On December 8, Congress declared war on Japan. Three days later, Germany and Italy declared war on the United States, bringing America into the war in Europe, too.

Being a wartime president brought new stresses. While Roosevelt's polio didn't affect his ability to make decisions, more serious health problems occasionally interfered with his job.

In late November 1943, he traveled to Tehran, Iran, to discuss the war in Europe with the major U.S. allies—Winston Churchill of the United Kingdom and Joseph Stalin of the Soviet Union. The journey was exhausting, and soon after returning home, Roosevelt came down with influenza. By January, he had developed bronchitis, a bad cough, and a sinus infection. People noticed that he'd lost weight and was gaunt.

Yet on January 30, 1944, Roosevelt's sixty-second birthday, Dr. McIntire reported that the president "was in better health than at any time since he has been in the White House." McIntire claimed Roosevelt had recovered from the flu, thanks to his "above-average stamina." The doctor dismissed

In one of the few photographs of Roosevelt in his wheelchair, he poses in 1941 at Top Cottage, his retreat near his Hyde Park home. His cousin Margaret Suckley took the photo, which includes his dog Fala and the daughter of the cottage caretakers.

In *Life* magazine's August 16, 1937, issue, a photograph showed Roosevelt being pushed in his wheelchair. The White House usually succeeded in preventing such photographs from being taken or published. But *Life*'s editor Henry Luce was politically opposed to Roosevelt, and he wasn't deterred by the White House rules.

The President is here shown on his way to visit a sick Cabinet member at the old-fashioned Naval Hospital on E Street. Built in 1902, the Hospital has only 178 beds. Government officials are admitted only on the President's order, must pay for their subsistence.

This photograph shows the back of Roosevelt in his wheelchair on his terrace at Hyde Park in September 1937.

the weight loss that was so apparent to others, saying the president was back to his normal weight again. Those around Roosevelt could see this was untrue.

Roosevelt's daughter, Anna, was living at the White House with her husband and young son. Unlike her mother, who often traveled, Anna saw her father every day. By the end of March 1944, she was alarmed. Roosevelt looked haggard, and his cough hadn't improved. Anna didn't accept Dr. McIntire's explanation that her father just needed time in the sun to get back to normal. She asked the doctor to arrange a complete medical examination at the Naval Hospital.

McIntire agreed to set up an appointment with Dr. Howard Bruenn, a respected young naval cardiologist. Besides finding that the president's lungs hadn't cleared up from his bronchitis, Bruenn discovered that he had high blood pressure and a damaged, enlarged heart. This condition made it difficult for his heart to pump blood through his body.

Checking Roosevelt's past medical records, Bruenn learned that his patient had been suffering from high blood pressure for at least seven years. He didn't understand why Dr. McIntire hadn't brought in a cardiologist sooner.

In 1944, there were no effective drug treatments for high blood pressure. Bruenn recommended complete bedrest for one or two weeks, a lower salt intake (salt was known to increase blood pressure), and a diet to reduce his weight (alleviating the strain on his heart). He also gave Roosevelt digitalis.

Roosevelt smoked as many as forty cigarettes a day. To relieve his coughing, Bruenn advocated cutting back to six. In 1944, the medical community hadn't yet realized that tobacco use could lead to lung cancer, strokes, and heart attacks.

McIntire invited several other well-known doctors to consult. The group agreed to Bruenn's plan. While total bedrest was impossible in the middle of a world war, Roosevelt did reduce each workday to four hours.

After Bruenn's examination, McIntire told reporters that the president's only medical troubles were minor—a sinus infection and bronchitis, both on the mend. "For a man of 62 plus we had very little to argue about," said McIntire. He never mentioned the enlarged heart. He didn't release details from the exam, such as the blood pressure reading.

Because of Roosevelt's newly diagnosed heart issues, McIntire assigned Dr. Bruenn to the White House. The cardiologist also traveled with the president. But McIntire instructed Bruenn not to tell the press, the president, or his family anything about Roosevelt's health. Instead, McIntire took charge of relaying that information. Although Bruenn never discussed his diagnosis with the president, Roosevelt later revealed to others that he knew his heart and blood pressure were problems.

In April, McIntire and Bruenn recommended a break from the White House. Roosevelt spent a month at the South Carolina winter home of one of his advisors. His bronchitis cleared, and the digitalis improved his heart function. After the trip, the president felt better.

A FOURTH TERM

On June 6, 1944, Allied forces (American, British, Canadian) invaded western Europe at the beaches of Normandy in France. D-Day had been a long-planned operation to push back the German army. Roosevelt was relieved when it went well, despite the loss of Allied lives. This action marked a major step toward the Allies' defeat of Hitler's Germany.

Roosevelt looked ahead to the 1944 presidential election. At the Democrats' July convention, they would be nominating their candidates for the November vote. Most in the party agreed that the U.S. president needed to be seen by the enemy, as well as by the American public, as strong and in control. Dr. McIntire headed off concerns about Roosevelt's vigor. He announced to the press that the president's health was "excellent in all respects." McIntire said it was "better than the average for a man of his age."

Some Democratic Party leaders didn't buy McIntire's statements. Roosevelt had aged considerably. His facial skin sagged. He had dark rings under his eyes. One of those politicians later admitted that he and others were aware that the president's health had declined. The man wrote in a letter to the *New York Times*, "It was widely known among political leaders that he [Roosevelt] was a dying man." Members of Roosevelt's family and several friends didn't think he could withstand a fourth term, either.

Nobody asked Dr. Bruenn about Roosevelt's health, though he was sure Democratic leaders and White House advisors who saw him by the president's side knew that he was a cardiologist.

But Roosevelt refused to quit while the war was still raging. He intended to run again, and in July, the Democratic Party nominated him for his fourth term. To be safe, party leaders carefully chose a vice presidential nominee with whom they could work if Roosevelt died. Harry Truman got the nod. As a U.S. senator since 1935, he had supported Roosevelt's

A campaign poster from 1944 when Roosevelt ran for his fourth term. No other president had been elected more than twice. The United States was in the middle of World War II, and the majority of voters decided to stick with Roosevelt despite concerns about his health.

policies and been effective at getting things done in the Senate. He was from Missouri and could bring Midwestern votes to the ticket.

During the fall campaign, Roosevelt made a point of appearing hardy. He even rode in an open car during a rainstorm to greet voters in New York City. His aides discouraged close-up photographs, and the press usually went along.

Roosevelt's deteriorated condition was obvious anyway. Rumors that had been simmering for several years began to surface again: The president had had a series of strokes. He had been secretly treated for cancer. He'd had a heart attack.

The Democratic national chairman accused "the people who don't want Roosevelt" of waging "a whispering campaign" about his health.

The president responded to the numerous "whispers" by telling reporters at his regular news conference that "he was in pretty good health."

The whispers grew louder, however. The *Chicago Daily Tribune* charged in its October 17 edition that the president's health was "one of the principal issues of this campaign." The evidence was that he "is not in fit physical condition to meet [the] demands" of the presidency. That evidence included his frequent time away from his office, photographs showing a frail man, and his radio voice that sounded weaker.

The August 1944 Gallup poll found that a third of all voters thought Roosevelt's health would not allow him to carry on for four additional years. Among Democratic voters, 84 percent were confident that he could handle a fourth term, but only 16 percent of Republicans believed that.

When the voting was over on November 7, Roosevelt had won. Still, his margin of victory over his Republican challenger, Thomas Dewey, was the narrowest of his four presidential elections.

WARM SPRINGS

After Roosevelt's inauguration on January 20, 1945, he left for another meeting with Churchill and Stalin, this time in Yalta, Crimea, in the Soviet Union. The Allies were now confident of victory in Europe. The purpose of the Yalta Conference was to discuss how to deal with Germany and the countries of eastern Europe after the war ended.

In February 1945, as World War II in Europe was winding down, the leaders of the major Western Allies met in Yalta to discuss the war's aftermath. From the left: Winston Churchill of the United Kingdom, Roosevelt, and Joseph Stalin of the Soviet Union. In this photograph, Churchill is smoking a cigar and Roosevelt (a heavy smoker) holds a cigarette. By this time, the president looked pale and infirm.

Diplomats who met with Roosevelt noticed how feeble he looked. At times, he seemed unable to focus on the conversation. When Roosevelt returned from Yalta and met with his vice president, Truman "was shocked by his appearance. His eyes were sunken. His magnificent smile was missing from his careworn face. He seemed a spent man."

On March 1, Roosevelt visited the Capitol to report on the Yalta Conference. He entered the Chamber of the House of Representatives pushed in his wheelchair. In all previous appearances before Congress, he had worn his braces and "walked" as he held someone's arm. After his wheelchair reached the front of the Chamber, Roosevelt shifted himself to a chair behind a table that faced the audience of senators and representatives. It was the first time he spoke to Congress while seated.

That wasn't the only unprecedented moment. As the president began his one-hour speech, he mentioned his leg braces. "I hope that you will pardon me for an unusual posture of sitting down during the presentation of what I want to say, but I know that you will realize that it makes it a lot easier for me in not having to carry about ten pounds of steel 'round on the bottom of my legs."

The radio announcer told listeners at home, "He looks in excellent health. He looks excellent." Those who saw him in person disagreed. "Plainly, he was a very weary man," Vice President Truman recalled. People who heard his voice over the radio thought the speech lacked the president's typical energy and smooth delivery.

Roosevelt's reference to his paralysis raised questions. One reporter wrote, "For more than 12 years, without any specific taboos, there has been an understanding that no stories or pictures would be circulated playing on Mr. Roosevelt's infirmity." Why start now? The reporter found an answer while interviewing Roosevelt's political and personal friends. In their opinion, the president did not plan to run for office ever again and no longer felt that he had to hide his disability.

The secrecy over the years paid off. Many Americans still believed Roosevelt had long ago recovered from his polio and paralysis. They didn't know that he could only stand with braces and for a limited amount of time. They didn't recognize that when he walked, he was supported by the person whose arm he clutched. They weren't aware that he had to be carried up stairs and lifted out of a car.

After the speech, Dr. Bruenn was concerned by Roosevelt's appearance. He decided his patient needed total rest to recuperate from his Yalta trip. On March 29, Roosevelt traveled to Warm Springs with Bruenn. Dr. McIntire stayed in Washington.

The vacation at Roosevelt's cottage relaxed him. He enjoyed the company of a few friends and two of his cousins. His appetite improved, and he put on weight. On April 10, he told McIntire over the phone, "You're going to like the way I look and the way I feel."

On Thursday morning, April 12, the president worked on government papers while an artist sketched him for a watercolor painting. About 1:00 p.m., before lunch was served, Roosevelt suddenly lifted his hand and said, "I have a terrific pain in the back of my head."

He collapsed, unconscious.

Two aides carried Roosevelt to his bed. His cousin called for Dr. Bruenn, who arrived in fifteen minutes. After examining the president, Bruenn realized that he'd had a massive cerebral hemorrhage—a stroke. A blood vessel had broken, causing bleeding in his brain. There was nothing Bruenn could do. At 3:35 p.m., Roosevelt took his final breath without regaining consciousness.

In Washington, Eleanor was informed of her husband's death. She requested that there be no autopsy. The death certificate, signed by Bruenn,

listed cerebral hemorrhage as the cause of death and arteriosclerosis as a contributing cause.

Shortly after seven that evening, the chief justice of the Supreme Court administered the oath of office to Vice President Truman in the Cabinet Room of the White House. About twenty other people were present, including cabinet members, congressional leaders, and Truman's wife and daughter. Like Chester Arthur, Truman (1945–1953) would have no vice president for the nearly four years remaining in the presidential term.

Franklin Roosevelt's casket was taken to Washington by train, and a private service was held in the White House East Room on April 14. The next day a train carried his body to his Hyde Park estate, where he was buried in the rose garden.

The last photograph taken of Roosevelt, on April 11, 1945. The photographer shot it for Elizabeth Shoumatoff, an artist who was painting Roosevelt's portrait in Warm Springs, Georgia. The president died the next day, and the portrait remained unfinished.

Within three weeks of Roosevelt's death, Hitler committed suicide and Germany surrendered. On May 8, the war in Europe ended.

Harry Truman had not been part of Roosevelt's inner circle, and the late president had kept him in the dark about important topics. Fearing that the Germans were developing atomic weapons, the United States had secretly started its own nuclear research program. Although the work continued throughout the war, Truman never knew about it until he became president. In August 1945, America detonated two atomic bombs over Japan, bringing the fighting there to a conclusion. World War II was finally over.

THE TRUTH COMES OUT

On the same day that the *New York Times* announced Roosevelt's death, it ran an article, "Roosevelt Health Long Under Doubt." With the president dead, journalists no longer felt that they had to stay quiet about his health. The *Times* article alleged that official statements for two years "appeared to be in conflict with visible evidences of his physical condition." The White House had deliberately lied to the public.

A year later, Dr. McIntire wrote a book defending himself. He asserted that he had never been deceptive in his press statements. The extensive medical exams during the last two years of the president's life, he said, proved that Roosevelt was in "excellent condition for a man of his age." According to McIntire, the only thing wrong with Roosevelt was moderate arteriosclerosis, which wasn't unusual for a sixty-three-year-old in a stressful job. The doctor claimed that neither Roosevelt's blood pressure nor his arteriosclerosis was serious enough to predict his fatal stroke.

McIntire wasn't being honest. The truth didn't emerge until 1970 when Dr. Bruenn published his medical notes, with the blessing of Roosevelt's children. He recounted his examinations and tests of the president starting in March 1944 until Roosevelt's death in April 1945. For the first time, the public learned about Roosevelt's enlarged heart and excessively high blood pressure. Despite what McIntire repeatedly told reporters, the president had not been "in splendid shape."

Bruenn wrote that he was making his account public for the historical record. Otherwise, no one would know the facts because the president's medical file had mysteriously disappeared from a safe at the Naval Hospital.

Historians have investigated the missing records. They concluded that Dr. McIntire likely removed them soon after the president's death, either to protect Roosevelt's privacy or to cover up his own failure to properly treat his patient. The speculation about heart attacks, small strokes, and an underlying cancer can never be verified because those medical records vanished and there was no autopsy.

A few weeks after Roosevelt's death, *The Saturday Evening Post* magazine published an editorial called, "Everybody Knew it But the People." It pointed out that "the state of Mr. Roosevelt's health was a secret from millions of Americans who voted for the President on the theory that he could reasonably be expected to live out his term of office." Even though the president was ill, those close to him worked hard to keep that secret. The editorial concluded, "It must not happen again."

But it *did* happen again.

JOHN KENNEDY

BORN: May 29, 1917, in Brookline, Massachusetts

PROFESSION BEFORE PRESIDENCY: Navy lieutenant, U.S. congressman and senator from Massachusetts

POLITICAL PARTY: Democrat

ELECTED: 1960

SERVED: January 1961 to November 1963

DIED: November 22, 1963, Dallas, Texas, age forty-six

PRESIDENTIAL TRIVIA:

★ Kennedy was the first president born in the twentieth century and the first Catholic to hold the office.

★ At age forty-three, Kennedy was the youngest elected president and the youngest at the end of his term. (Theodore Roosevelt, who was vice president in 1901, took office at age forty-two after President William McKinley was assassinated.)

John Fitzgerald Kennedy in 1961, the year he became president

CHAPTER SEVEN

TARNISHED HERO

"I'm the healthiest candidate for President in the country, and I'm not going to die in office."
—JOHN KENNEDY

NOT SO HEALTHY

JOHN FITZGERALD KENNEDY WAS USED TO NEEDLES JABBING HIM. HE WAS used to surgeons' scalpels slicing into his flesh. He was used to hospital beds. He was used to excruciating pain. And during his entire political career leading to the presidency, he was used to keeping it all a secret. Now that he was finally in the White House, the truth remained hidden.

Kennedy successfully concealed his suffering behind a dazzling smile and outgoing personality. The public knew him as a tall, attractive man with thick reddish-brown hair and perfect white teeth who was just forty-three years old. He appeared athletic, energetic, and healthy.

Few people realized that John Kennedy was one of the country's sickliest presidents.

Jack, as he was called, was the second of nine children born to a wealthy Massachusetts family involved in politics. His businessman father served in President Franklin Roosevelt's administration as ambassador to the United Kingdom. His maternal grandfather had been Boston's mayor and a member of the U.S. House of Representatives.

Young Jack seemed to catch every childhood illness, and he didn't recover quickly. As a toddler, he was hospitalized for more than two months with scarlet fever. Before antibiotics became widely available in the late 1940s, that disease could damage the heart, ears, and eyes, and even kill a child.

When he was thirteen, Jack lost weight. He felt tired and occasionally dizzy. Doctors weren't sure what was wrong. A month before he turned fourteen, he developed severe abdominal pains. A doctor diagnosed appendicitis and removed Jack's appendix. Yet the pain returned.

During his junior year at a private boarding high school, Jack was bedridden with stomachaches and diarrhea for part of the year. After a similar attack when he was eighteen, doctors decided he had either hepatitis or jaundice—both liver ailments—because his skin turned yellow. The same symptoms stuck with him into college, interfering with his education every time they flared up.

Jack's parents sent him to several hospitals for tests and treatments. Doctors finally diagnosed colitis, a painful inflammation of the large intestine. They advised him to eat a bland diet of food that was easy to digest, staying away from spices, raw vegetables, and alcohol.

By the time Jack graduated from Harvard University in 1940, he had another medical issue—an aching back. He began wearing a cloth brace around his middle to support his spine. One of his doctors later said he believed Jack had been born with a weak back. But the ambitious Kennedy family didn't want the hint of a physical imperfection to interfere with Jack's success in life. Jack claimed that his back problems started with a college football injury.

As war in Europe raged and a wider conflict looked likely, Kennedy decided to enlist in the military the way his older brother and friends were doing. His many illnesses and bad back disqualified him. His father had political influence in Washington, however. By early fall 1941, he had arranged for Jack to get a position in the U.S. Navy.

On December 7, 1941, the Japanese bombed Pearl Harbor, Hawaii, and the United States entered World War II. The navy sent Kennedy to the South Pacific and assigned him the command of a small attack craft, called a patrol torpedo boat, or PT boat. In August 1943, Kennedy's *PT-109* was rammed by a Japanese destroyer, killing two of his crew. When their damaged boat began to sink hours later, he and the remaining men swam toward land. Kennedy towed one severely injured crew member by the man's life vest. The eleven men survived for several days on an island until they were rescued.

Lieutenant John F. Kennedy in the cockpit of the World War II patrol torpedo boat, *PT-109*. In August 1943, a Japanese destroyer rammed the boat, killing two men and marooning the survivors for nearly a week until they were rescued.

Weeks after the rescue, Kennedy landed in a navy hospital suffering from malaria, colitis, and back pain made worse by the *PT-109* ordeal. Doctors sent him home to the States where he had back surgery in the summer of 1944. The operation didn't relieve his pain as surgeons hoped. To treat his discomfort, doctors injected the anesthetic procaine. The injections helped numb the pain, but only temporarily.

While Jack was recovering from his back surgery in August 1944, his older brother, Joe, was killed while piloting a navy bomber plane. The Kennedy family had expected Joe to enter Democratic Party politics. Jack stepped into that role after the navy discharged him in 1945 because of his colitis and back problems.

In 1946, Kennedy ran for a seat in the U.S. House of Representatives from Massachusetts. With support from his family's contacts and influence, Kennedy campaigned hard ahead of the November election. His poor health sometimes got in the way. He was often fatigued. His stomach and intestinal ailments continued, and he was significantly underweight for his six-foot (2 m) frame. Kennedy took medications for his colitis, but those didn't always relieve his symptoms. To soothe his painful back, he soaked in a hot water bath every day.

His campaign hid his physical problems from the voters, and Kennedy won his first election.

DEFECTIVE GLANDS

In 1947, during the fall of Kennedy's first year in Congress, he visited England. While there, he became seriously ill, vomiting and running a fever. He was too weak to stand.

The doctor who treated him at a London hospital told Kennedy that he had Addison's disease. It was the first time anyone had suggested this condition to explain the symptoms Kennedy had had for years: weakness, fatigue, poor appetite, nausea, diarrhea, vomiting, weight loss, and tan or yellow skin. Back in the United States, a Boston physician confirmed the Addison's diagnosis.

Addison's is caused when the adrenal glands fail to produce enough important hormones. These hormones regulate blood pressure, the immune system, heart function, and the body's response to stress. Addison's was once considered a fatal disease. In 1939, researchers developed a synthetic replacement for the missing hormones, allowing Addison's patients to live with the condition.

Kennedy began treatment with a pellet of this medication implanted under his skin every three months. Later he added a daily oral dose of the steroid hormone cortisone. For the rest of his life, he needed the hormone substitutes to survive.

Kennedy kept his Addison's diagnosis a secret. To explain why he'd been hospitalized, he told reporters that he'd had a recurrence of the malaria he caught in the South Pacific during the war. His skin looked yellow, he said, because that was a symptom of malaria. The press printed his story, reminding newspaper readers that Kennedy was a war hero.

After serving three terms in Congress, Jack Kennedy ran for the U.S. Senate in 1952. His family helped drum up support for his candidacy, and his younger brother Robert managed the campaign. When Jack experienced his usual back pain and stomach and intestinal issues, doctors prescribed medications to relax the muscles of his back and digestive tract. Behind the scenes, Kennedy was suffering, but the public saw a young, handsome, and tireless candidate.

Kennedy won, upsetting a Republican who had held the Senate seat for two terms. The next fall, he married Jacqueline Bouvier. They later had two children, Caroline and John. Two other children were born prematurely and didn't live.

Meanwhile, the vertebrae in Kennedy's lower back were deteriorating. He was in constant pain and could barely walk without crutches. Doctors told him that he needed surgery to stabilize his damaged spine. Otherwise, he'd soon have to depend on a wheelchair to move around.

Surgeons hesitated to operate on a patient with Addison's. The disease reduced the body's ability to deal with stress and infection, making surgery dangerous. Despite the risk of death, Kennedy opted to have the operation rather than lose his ability to walk at age thirty-seven.

The Kennedy team informed the press that he required surgery to fix the injury he received when his PT boat was destroyed. There was no mention of his back problems *before* the war or his Addison's disease. Once again, Kennedy's physical weakness was turned into a symbol of valor.

The October 1954 surgery was difficult because the doctors had to use drugs to compensate for Kennedy's faulty adrenal glands. Though he came through the three-hour operation, he developed an infection soon afterward and almost died. Antibiotics saved him, but in four months he needed another surgery to make more repairs.

By the time Kennedy had recovered enough to return to his Senate office in May 1955, he had missed eight months of Senate business. A Washington newspaper headline read "Kennedy, Tan and Fit, Returns to His Office." The senator told reporters that he no longer needed crutches, and most people thought that his surgery had cured his back problems. In fact, Kennedy couldn't put on his socks or walk down steps without help.

Shortly after his return to the Senate, he sought help from a New York expert in chronic pain, Dr. Janet Travell. She eventually became his personal physician. Travell realized that Kennedy's left leg was slightly shorter than his right, which created a strain on his skeleton with every step. She had him add a lift to all his left-foot shoes. Travell suggested that he use a cushioned rocking chair instead of a regular chair because it took the pressure off his lower back. For spinal support, he wore an 8-inch-wide (20 cm) canvas belt around his middle.

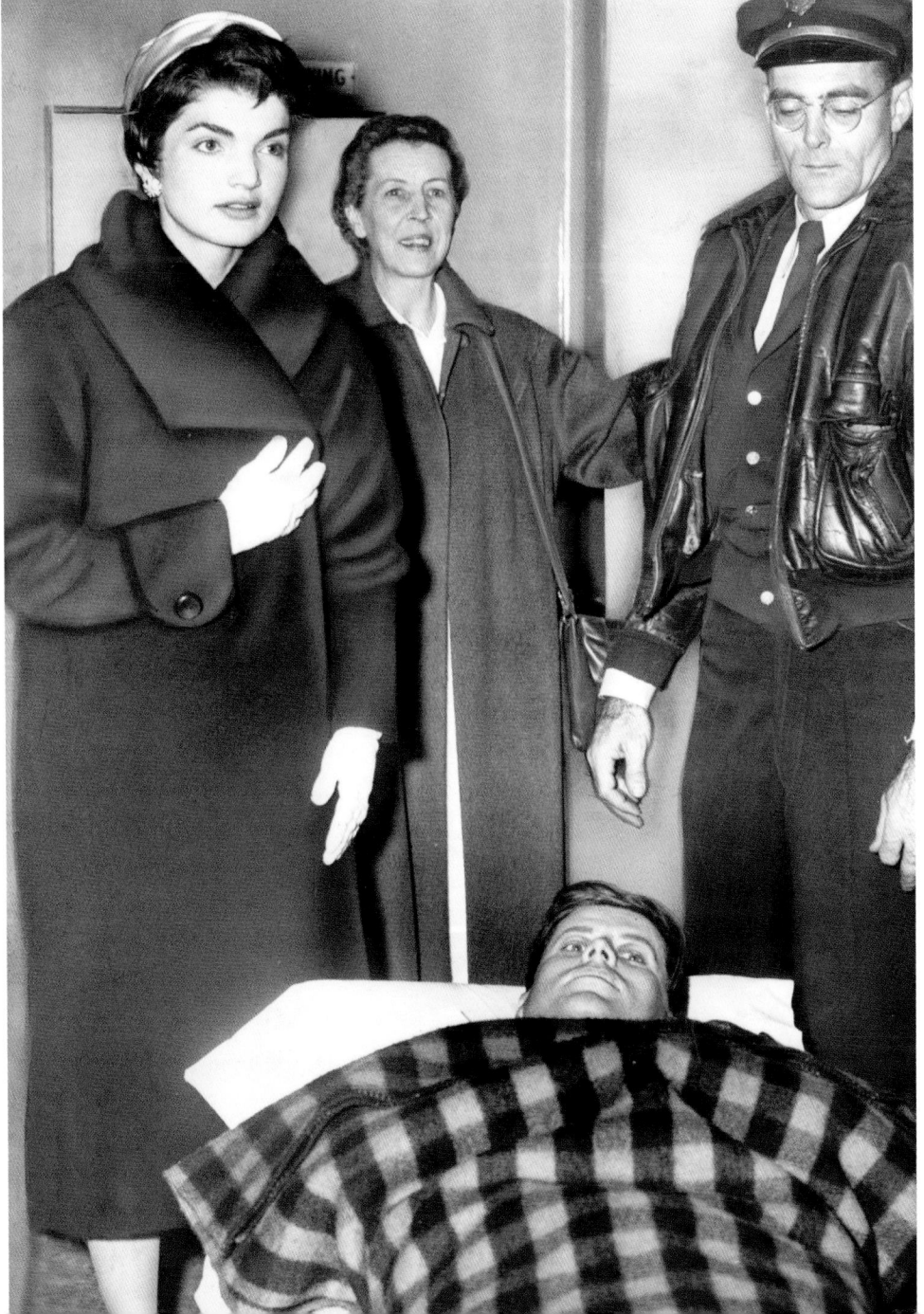

Senator John Kennedy leaves a New York hospital in December 1954 after back surgery, accompanied by his wife, Jacqueline (left). He was absent from the Senate for eight months because of surgeries.

Senator Kennedy's health issues weren't over. Between May 1955 and October 1957, he was in the hospital nine times for a range of ailments: excruciating back pain, colitis and diarrhea, urinary tract and throat infections, an abscess, fever, vomiting, weight loss. He concealed these stays, using an alias to check into the hospitals.

His brother Robert later wrote, "At least one half of the days that he spent on this earth were days of intense physical pain." By all accounts, Jack didn't complain.

RACE FOR PRESIDENT

Despite his medical problems, Kennedy pushed forward in his quest for the White House. Not believing that any of his ailments would interfere with a president's duties, he set his eye on the 1960 election.

Still, he was concerned that he might be politically vulnerable should the public learn about his health, especially Addison's. Even though the condition could now be controlled with replacement hormones, he didn't want voters to connect him with a formerly fatal disease. There were already rumors. Kennedy had lied when he was diagnosed with Addison's in 1947, saying that he had malaria. He had to keep up the lie.

In mid-July 1959, one of Kennedy's advisors asked him about those rumors. Was it true that his adrenal glands didn't work properly and he took cortisone? Kennedy replied, "No one who has the real Addison's disease should run for the Presidency, but I do not have it."

Dr. Travell helped Kennedy hide the truth by relabeling his condition. Later that July, she wrote a statement for him to use when anyone, including reporters, asked about his health. Her statement explained that the stress of the *PT-109* incident and malaria caused "a

depletion of adrenal function from which he is now fully rehabilitated."
By connecting the ailment to his war experience, she emphasized
his heroism.

Travell implied that Kennedy had just a minor disorder, an "adrenal insufficiency," not Addison's disease. She made it sound as if Kennedy had recovered. In fact, his condition couldn't be cured. He needed hormone supplements to survive.

Another misleading sentence in the statement claimed that Kennedy had "above-average resistance to infections." Historians later uncovered medical records showing that he was prone to infections and frequently took the antibiotic penicillin.

Travell wrote that Kennedy's "back is entirely well" and that his pain was gone. Yet the back problems had *not* disappeared, and he still required painkillers.

A year later, at the July 1960 Democratic Party convention, Kennedy's opponent for the party's nomination was Senator Lyndon Johnson of Texas. Kennedy's allies brought up Johnson's heart attack five years before, suggesting that Kennedy was more fit for the job.

Johnson had heard the rumors about Kennedy's medical history. Two of his aides publicly charged that John Kennedy was hardly the robust man he claimed to be. They accused him of suffering from Addison's disease and depending on cortisone to stay alive.

Kennedy fought back. If too many voters thought he was seriously ill, it could keep him out of the White House.

His team put out a new medical statement from Dr. Travell and Dr. Eugene Cohen, the doctor who treated Kennedy's "adrenal insufficiency," as they called it. The statement repeated Travell's 1959 report and added that Kennedy didn't take cortisone.

Their words were deceptive. Kennedy had taken cortisone earlier for his Addison's disease. But by 1960, he had switched to regular doses of a chemical relative of cortisone. The rest of the statement was intentionally vague, making people think that Kennedy had been cured. Kennedy's press secretary was clearer. He told reporters "that the Kennedy illness was a thing of the past."

The campaign's response to the Johnson camp quelled concerns about Kennedy's health, and he went on to win the nomination. To gain the backing of the southern Democrats and strengthen the ticket, he made Lyndon Johnson his vice-presidential running mate.

The fall campaign pitted Kennedy against the Republican's nominee, Vice President Richard Nixon. Kennedy exploited the image of a young, dynamic candidate, a contrast to the retiring seventy-year-old President Dwight Eisenhower (1953–1961), who, at the time, was the oldest president ever to serve.

Kennedy's flyers and brochures urged voters to cast their ballots for the candidate who offered "Youth and Vigor." His four televised debates with Nixon solidified this image. Although Kennedy was just four years younger than his opponent, he was far more photogenic than Nixon.

The Kennedy team had managed to stop the Addison's disease story from gaining traction in the press. But several days before the election, John Roosevelt, son of the late President Franklin Roosevelt, called on both Kennedy and Nixon to release their complete medical records.

Roosevelt stated that because the fate of the world could "depend on the health and judgment of the American president," voters should know the candidates' true physical condition. He was well aware that his father's health status had been kept hidden when he ran for a fourth term in 1944. Roosevelt advocated for a law that required presidential candidates to

The four debates between presidential candidates John Kennedy and Richard Nixon were the first ever to be televised. The third one, on October 13, 1960, was shown on a split screen with Nixon in Los Angeles (left) and Kennedy in New York City. The men appeared in person together for the other three debates. Though Nixon lost the 1960 election, he would later become president himself (1969–1974).

have a medical exam and to make the results public. Fortunately for Kennedy, nothing came of Roosevelt's appeal.

On election night, the vote was too close to call. The next day, results showed that Kennedy had won the popular vote by less than 0.2 percent. Leading Republicans wanted Nixon to challenge the results in some states. But he declined to ask for recounts because he thought they would take too

KENNEDY WINS PRESIDENCY

Nixon Concedes Kennedy Victory As Jack's Electoral Vote Hits 272

The Weather
Today—Cloudy with occasional rain; high near 60 degrees. Tonight—Clear ing, considerably colder; low about 32. Friday—Fair and colder. Wednesday's temperatures: High, 50 at 3:45 p m.; low, 34 at 6:55 a.m. Details, Page B12.

The Washington Post FINAL
Times Herald

83rd Year · · · No. 341   Phone RE. 7-1234 Copyright 1960. The Washington Post Co.   THURSDAY, NOVEMBER 10, 1960   WTOP Radio (1500) TV (Ch. 9)   TEN CENTS

Republicans Concede Kennedy Victory; Vote Edge Drops to Less Than 325,000

Kennedy Apparently Next President

Headlines after the November 1960 presidential election (in order from top): *Chicago Daily Tribune*; *Evening Press* [Binghamton, NY]; *Washington Post*; *Burlington* [VT] *Free Press*. The popular vote was so close that the results weren't known until the day after the election. Although Nixon conceded then, questions have lingered about voter fraud in Chicago and Texas.

long, leaving the country without leadership for months. Nixon conceded the afternoon after the election.

John Kennedy had achieved his goal. He became the youngest elected president in U.S. history.

At a press conference later that week, a reporter asked Kennedy about his physical condition, specifically his back and Addison's disease. Kennedy replied, "I have never had the matter to which you referred, Addison's disease." He added that his back was cleared up in 1955 and was "no problem."

Neither statement was true.

President Kennedy with his children, four-year-old
Caroline and nineteen-month-old John Jr., and Macaroni
the Pony at the White House on June 22, 1962

PILLS AND INJECTIONS

A few days before Kennedy took the oath of office on January 20, 1961, a popular medical magazine published an article about his health. National newspapers later quoted parts of it. The author had interviewed Dr. Janet Travell and Kennedy's brother Robert. Much of the profile echoed the misinformation put out by Kennedy's team for years.

The article painted him as a determined hero who overcame medical challenges. He'd had some illnesses as a youth, but Kennedy was now in excellent health. His temporary adrenal insufficiency was gone. Although he took a replacement hormone, it was only as insurance against the condition's return. He'd never had Addison's disease. His back was completely well.

Readers were told that he was "not much of a pill man. He scorns pep pills, and doesn't feel the need of even an aspirin tablet." In summary, the president had been "free of health problems the past year."

This was far from accurate.

Dr. Travell followed Kennedy to the White House as his personal physician, and historians have since examined her records. During Kennedy's first ten months as president, he was often taking more than a

On June 22, 1961, Kennedy's personal physician, Dr. Janet Travell, addresses the press after the president unexpectedly canceled his daily appointments. Press secretary Pierre Salinger stands beside her. She explained that Kennedy was recovering from a mild infection that caused a sore throat and fever, and she had given him antibiotics. When asked whether he was taking drugs for his adrenal insufficiency, she responded that he only took them occasionally. In truth, Kennedy took the medication daily.

dozen medications a day. These were to treat stomach cramps, diarrhea, urinary tract infections, allergies, unintended weight loss, and back pain. In addition, he took daily medication for his Addison's disease. One of Kennedy's close aides later wrote that when the president traveled, he took along "more pills, potions, poultices and other paraphernalia than would be found in a small dispensary."

While visiting Canada in May 1961, Kennedy strained his back when he planted a ceremonial tree. Left with continuous pain, he had trouble climbing stairs, bending over, and rising from a chair. Occasionally, he needed crutches. To relieve the agony, Dr. Travell injected his back with procaine two or three times a day.

In the same period, Kennedy was getting back injections from Dr. Max Jacobson, a New York doctor he had started seeing during the presidential campaign. Jacobson, called Dr. Feelgood by his patients, was known for treating celebrities with his own concoction of painkillers and amphetamines. Amphetamines (pep pills) are stimulant drugs that speed up the body's systems. They can be addictive.

White House records show that Jacobson visited more than thirty times before May 1962 and continued treating

After straining his back in May 1961, President Kennedy needed crutches to walk. He avoided using them in public. Photo from June 16, 1961.

Kennedy into that fall. Dr. Feelgood even traveled to Europe with the president. Kennedy was convinced that whatever Jacobson was giving him helped his back feel better.

Navy doctor George Burkley, a member of the White House medical staff, was also assigned to care for the president. He and Dr. Travell clashed about the daily procaine injections she was giving Kennedy. Burkley believed that the body could get accustomed to procaine, requiring increasing amounts to lessen the pain.

He arranged for an expert on physical therapy, Dr. Hans Kraus of New York City, to come to Washington to treat Kennedy's back. Kraus designed a program that involved swimming and doing specific exercises every day to build up the muscles of the president's back and abdomen. Kraus told Kennedy that if he didn't follow the regimen, he would end up permanently in a wheelchair. This apparently scared the president into working with the doctor.

Burkley and Kraus helped relieve Kennedy's painful back spasms with massages and heat. By spring 1962, as the president's back felt better and he moved more easily, Burkley and Kraus convinced him to stop Travell's

Kennedy depended on rocking chairs to reduce his back pain. At this October 1963 meeting in the White House, he speaks with the prime minister of Nyasaland (later called Malawi), in the middle, and the U.S. assistant secretary of state for African Affairs. The Kennedy team promoted the president's rocking chair as a "symbol of the traditional values, reflective patience and practical informality prevailing in the White House."

President Kennedy meets with civil rights leaders in the White House Oval Office on August 28, 1963. Earlier that day, Martin Luther King, Jr., (third from the left) gave his famous "I Have a Dream" speech at the March on Washington for Jobs and Freedom. The March was organized to rally support for economic and racial equality. Kennedy proposed a civil rights bill to Congress in June 1963, but he did not live to see it signed into law in July 1964.

procaine injections. Dr. Cohen, who had long treated the president's Addison's disease, agreed that Kennedy should not be getting the procaine shots.

Gradually, with Kennedy's consent, these doctors eased Travell out of her role. She stayed on as a White House physician, taking care of Jacqueline and the Kennedy children. But she was instructed not to medicate the president. Even though Kennedy made this decision, he sometimes asked Travell to give him procaine.

Concerned about the drugs the president was receiving from Max Jacobson, Dr. Kraus confronted Kennedy in December 1962. "No President with his finger on the red button [the power to authorize a nuclear bomb attack]," he told Kennedy, "has any business taking stuff like that." Kraus threatened to publicize the drug use if he found out that Kennedy got another injection from Jacobson.

The injections—if they continued—stayed secret.

A FATEFUL VISIT

In November 1963, Kennedy set off on a speaking tour in Texas. He hoped to boost his popularity there ahead of the 1964 presidential election.

On Friday, November 22, he and Jacqueline sat in the rear seat of the black presidential limousine, part of a motorcade driving through Dallas on the way to a luncheon appearance. Texas governor John Connally and his wife sat in front of them. The convertible top was down. Kennedy wanted the crowd along the street to get a clear view of him.

Suddenly at 12:30 p.m., two shots rang out. Witnesses saw Kennedy pitch forward in his seat, grabbing his throat. Governor Connally was hit, too. Seconds later, a third bullet struck Kennedy in the head. Blood and brains from his wound splattered Jacqueline's pink suit.

The rifle shots had come from a sixth-floor window of a nearby building.

The limousine sped to Parkland Memorial Hospital four miles (6.4 km) away. A team of emergency room doctors and nurses went to work on the president, trying to save his life. It was too late. The final gunshot had blown his head apart. John Kennedy was pronounced dead at 1:00 p.m. Central Time.

Reporters immediately spread the tragic news around the world. People everywhere were stunned. No U.S. president had been assassinated since William McKinley in 1901, sixty years earlier.

Arrangements were made to fly Kennedy's body back to Washington on Air Force One as soon as possible. Vice President Lyndon Johnson, who had been in another car in the motorcade during the shooting, joined Jacqueline and Kennedy's aides on the plane. Before they took off from the Dallas

On November 22, 1963, President John Kennedy and the First Lady sit in the rear seat of a limousine as it drives through downtown Dallas. Texas Governor John Connally and his wife are in front of them. Minutes after this photograph was taken, the assassin's bullets struck and killed Kennedy and wounded Connally, who later recovered.

Two hours after Kennedy was shot, Lyndon
Johnson (1963–1969) took the oath of office
aboard Air Force One at a Dallas airport.
Johnson's wife, Lady Bird, stands to his right.
Jacqueline Kennedy, on his left, still wears
clothes soaked with her husband's blood.

airport, a Texas judge administered the presidential oath of office to Johnson at 2:38 p.m.

By then, police had arrested the presumed assassin, Lee Harvey Oswald, but not before he shot and killed a Dallas policeman. Oswald denied shooting the president.

Later that Friday night, navy pathologists performed an autopsy on President Kennedy's body at Bethesda Naval Hospital outside of Washington. The pathologists were told to determine only the cause of death. The Kennedy family did not want a complete autopsy in which all parts of the body are carefully examined. The pathologists concluded that two bullets had struck the president from behind. The fatal one entered his head.

PRESIDENT KENNEDY ASSASSINATED, DIES AT 2 P.M. IN DALLAS HOSPITAL

PRESIDENT ASSASSINATED

KENNEDY SHOT DEAD BY SNIPER DURING MOTORCADE IN DALLAS; JOHNSON SWORN IN AS PRESIDENT

Headlines announce Kennedy's assassination. The event shocked the nation and became an unforgettable moment in the lives of most Americans. The *Record* [East Bergen County, NJ] (top); *Ithaca* [NY] *Journal* (second from top); *Baltimore* [MD] *Sun* (bottom left); *Los Angeles Times* (bottom right).

Two days after Kennedy's assassination, police prepared to transfer Lee Harvey Oswald from the Dallas police headquarters to the county jail. A man named Jack Ruby stepped from a group in the headquarters hallway. While the nation watched on live television, Ruby shot Oswald in the abdomen at close range, killing him. For viewers reeling from Kennedy's death, it was another shock.

A special government commission investigated Kennedy's assassination and published its results nearly a year later. The report said that Oswald acted alone and that no one had hired Jack Ruby to shoot him. In the late 1970s, a separate congressional investigation reexamined the assassination. The committee members decided that, although Oswald shot Kennedy, he was likely part of a larger plot to murder the president. They weren't able to identify the others involved. For more than sixty years, conspiracy theories about Kennedy's assassination have continued to appear in books, articles, movies, and other media.

SECRETS REVEALED

John Kennedy's presidency lasted less than three years, during which he struggled every day with pain. For at least sixteen years, and probably longer, he had an incurable disease and needed medication to survive. He suffered with numerous other ailments that required drug treatment.

Kennedy, his family, and his doctors covered up his medical conditions as he climbed the ladder to the presidency, creating an image that was false. The cover-up went on after Kennedy's death. Robert Kennedy asked several doctors to destroy their records about his brother.

In 1992, the *Journal of the American Medical Association* (*JAMA*) interviewed one of the surgeons who operated on Kennedy's back in 1954. Along with three colleagues, the doctor had published a 1955 medical journal article discussing the challenges of operating on a man with Addison's disease. At the time of the surgery, their unidentified patient had had the condition for seven years and been on cortisone. Finally willing to break his silence after almost forty years, the surgeon confirmed what others had previously suspected: That patient was John Kennedy.

In other interviews with *JAMA* in 1992, members of the 1963 autopsy team revealed that they had examined some of Kennedy's organs. Based on the state of his adrenal glands, they verified that the assassinated president had severe Addison's disease, not a slight adrenal insufficiency as Dr. Travell claimed. This had not been included in the autopsy report.

The extent of John Kennedy's medical problems stayed secret for decades until the family allowed historians to review some of his records. Yet mysteries remain. Historians and physicians have speculated that Kennedy's many health issues might have been connected to an inherited autoimmune disorder. His sister Eunice also had Addison's disease, pointing to a hereditary explanation. But the records necessary to prove that either don't exist or are buried away.

Did any of Kennedy's ailments or their treatments impact his performance as president? No one can know for sure. But perhaps if the public had been aware of the truth about his health, Kennedy never would have been elected.

DIED IN OFFICE

THE NEXT IN LINE

The death of the president can lead to a national crisis. To maintain stability and ensure that the powers of the presidency continue uninterrupted, the framers of the Constitution added a vice president.

Article II, Section 1, Clause 6 directed this person to take over if the president died, resigned, was removed from office (after an impeachment, for example), or was unable to carry out presidential duties.

No presidents died in office until 1841, more than a half century after the Constitution went into effect. The ninth president, sixty-eight-year-old William Henry Harrison (1841), fell ill and died just one month after his inauguration. His vice president, John Tyler

John Tyler

(1841–1845), stepped up. But did Tyler become president? Or did he remain a vice president who carried out presidential responsibilities until the next election? The Constitution was unclear about that.

Tyler insisted that he had become president and was not an acting one. Congress went along with him.

After that, whenever a vice president had to take over, he was considered the president, not a temporary or acting one. This occurred seven more times after the deaths of Zachary Taylor (in 1850), Abraham Lincoln (in 1865), James Garfield (in 1881), William McKinley (in 1901), Warren Harding (in 1923), Franklin Roosevelt (in 1945), and John Kennedy (in 1963). It also happened when Richard Nixon resigned in 1974.

IF THE PRESIDENT AND VICE PRESIDENT ARE BOTH GONE . . .

There was another situation that the Constitution didn't spell out. What if both offices of the president and vice president are empty?

The Constitution gave Congress the power to handle that issue, and it did in 1792. The first Presidential Succession Act put two people in line to succeed the president and vice president—the president pro tempore of the Senate and the speaker of the House of Representatives. This successor would only *act* as president until a special election replaced both president and vice president. The 1792 law was never needed.

After the assassination of President Garfield, Congress saw a problem with the line of succession. When Chester Arthur took over, the office of vice president became empty. For several weeks, so were the positions of Senate president pro tempore and House speaker because Congress hadn't yet voted in those leaders.

In 1886, Congress passed the second Presidential Succession Act. Instead of the president pro tempore and speaker succeeding the vice president, members of the cabinet were next in line, starting with the secretary of state. This kept the line of succession in the executive branch and included more people. The new law also eliminated the requirement of a special election if the offices of both president and vice president were vacant. The acting president would stay in power until the next regular presidential election.

In 1947, Congress rewrote this plan again in the third Presidential Succession Act. It made the speaker and president pro tempore, in that order, the successors directly after the vice president. Cabinet members followed. This change made sure that the vice president was first succeeded by two elected officials, not appointed ones. As with the 1886 law, a successor would only act as president until the next regularly scheduled election.

The 1947 law still applies today, though a successor to a vice president has never been needed.

IF THE PRESIDENT CAN'T DO THE JOB . . .

The Constitution didn't outline a strategy for coping with a disabled president, such as James Garfield after he was shot and Woodrow Wilson after his stroke. For months, Garfield and Wilson couldn't do their jobs. Yet their vice presidents hesitated to take control even though other people thought they should step in for the good of the country.

Who decides that the president is unable to serve and that power should transfer to the vice president? In the early 1880s, President Arthur asked Congress to provide an answer, but legislators didn't act.

By 1955, the world and the United States' role in it had changed. Nuclear weapons made the planet more dangerous. The president's responsibilities were greater. President Dwight Eisenhower, who had had a heart attack and a stroke, recognized that someone must always be in charge. He

wanted to avoid a repeat of the Woodrow Wilson fiasco.

Eisenhower organized a group of legal experts and political scientists to propose an amendment to the Constitution that would address presidential disability. The group submitted a suggested amendment to Congress, but it didn't win approval.

In the meantime, Eisenhower made an informal agreement with his vice president, Richard Nixon, and it was made public. If Eisenhower was in a coma or otherwise incapable of performing his duties, Nixon could decide whether to take over as acting president. Eisenhower would declare when he was ready to resume his presidential

President Dwight Eisenhower and his vice president, Richard Nixon, in 1958

responsibilities. Subsequent presidents John Kennedy and Lyndon Johnson used a similar informal agreement.

Kennedy's 1963 assassination motivated Congress to finally move forward with an amendment setting up formal rules for handling presidential disabilities. What if Kennedy's wound had not been fatal, and he had ended up with a brain injury that permanently prevented him from governing? What if Vice President Lyndon Johnson then died? It was possible; Johnson had already had a heart attack.

Historians, legal experts, and political scientists helped Congress draft the Presidential Disability and Succession Amendment. By July 1965, both houses of Congress had approved the amendment and sent it to the states for ratification, as the Constitution required. In February 1967, after three-quarters of the states (thirty-eight) ratified it, the Twenty-Fifth Amendment became part of the Constitution.

THE TWENTY-FIFTH AMENDMENT

The amendment has four sections.

Section 1 says that if the president dies, resigns, or is removed from office, the vice president automatically *becomes* president until the next election. This had been the practice since John Tyler in 1841, but it had never been official.

Section 2 states that if there is no vice president, the president nominates a replacement. The nominee must be confirmed by the majority of both the Senate and House of Representatives. This situation had already occurred several times when a vice president succeeded to the presidency and left his previous position empty, and when a vice president resigned or died in office.

After the Twenty-Fifth Amendment was ratified, Sections 1 and 2 were used three times.

In 1973, during President Nixon's administration, Vice President Spiro Agnew resigned after being charged with corruption. Based on Section 2, Nixon nominated Gerald Ford to fill the position of vice president. Congress approved it. In August 1974, Nixon resigned under the threat of impeachment. Vice President Ford (1974–1977) automatically became president, as Section 1 directs. He nominated Nelson Rockefeller as vice president, which Congress approved. Both men served until the next regular election.

Sections 3 and 4 focus on a president who is unable to carry out the duties of the office.

Section 3 applies when the president voluntarily decides to transfer authority to the vice president. This can be temporary, such as for a medical procedure if the president is under anesthesia.

Eisenhower had informally arranged for this situation with his vice president, but Section 3 finally provides formal guidelines for transferring power. The president must send a written statement declaring this intention to the next two officials in line after the vice president—the House speaker and the Senate president pro tempore. The vice president will act as chief executive until the president sends a second statement saying that he or she is able to resume presidential duties.

In 1985, President Ronald Reagan (1981–1989) followed this process when he had surgery on his colon, or large intestine. But he didn't formally invoke the amendment when he temporarily passed power to Vice President George H. W. Bush. In 2002 and 2007, President George W. Bush (2001–2009) was the first president to invoke Section 3. He knew he'd be under general anesthesia during his colonoscopies. Vice President Dick Cheney became acting president for a couple of hours each time. In 2021, President Joe Biden (2021–2025) transferred powers to Vice President Kamala Harris for about ninety minutes when he had a colonoscopy.

Section 4 was designed to prevent a scenario like the aftermath of Woodrow Wilson's stroke. It explains what to do if the president can't carry out his or her duties *and* can't or won't voluntarily transfer power to the vice president. In that case, the vice president and the majority of the cabinet may decide that the president is unable to govern. (Alternatively, the vice president and the majority of another group designated by Congress make that decision.) The vice president then becomes acting president. The president stays in office but has no power or authority.

Under Section 4, the president can take back power by notifying the speaker and president pro tempore that the inability to govern no longer exists, or that there had never been an inability. If the vice president and majority of cabinet officers (or the alternative group) disagree, Congress settles the dispute. Two-thirds of each house of Congress must vote to uphold the removal of the president's powers. Otherwise, the president regains control.

Section 4 has never been used.

The Twenty-Fifth Amendment failed to correct all the succession issues. Some critics charge that the amendment doesn't clarify what "inability" means. And it doesn't describe *how* to determine if the president can't do the job.

Some conditions, like a coma, are clear-cut. But what about dementia, mental illness, addiction, or impairment from a stroke? If a medical opinion is needed, who gives it? Although the White House Medical Unit provides advice when the Twenty-Fifth Amendment is used, should an independent panel of doctors examine the president, too? As history shows, the White House physician might not be forthcoming about the president's health.

The amendment's supporters argue that its flexibility makes it more useful in emergencies.

Critics also point out that the amendment doesn't offer a method to deal with a vice president who is unable to perform duties. Nor does it say what to do if both president and vice president are disabled. So far, Congress hasn't fixed this.

To help with some of these uncertainties, recent presidents and their vice presidents have discussed situations that would trigger the amendment's Sections 3 and 4. Their written plans explain the way power would be transferred . . . and when. The details of these agreements have remained secret.

THE WHITE HOUSE MEDICAL UNIT

Today the White House Medical Unit cares for the president, vice president, and their families. The group includes the president's personal physician. The military oversees this unit, which is staffed primarily with military members including doctors, nurses, and physician assistants. All are trained in trauma and emergency care. The president may also receive care from outside specialists in a particular medical field. The medical unit advises officials if the Twenty-Fifth Amendment is used.

RONALD REAGAN

40th PRESIDENT

BORN: February 6, 1911, in Tampico, Illinois

PROFESSION BEFORE PRESIDENCY: radio sports announcer, television and movie actor, president of the Screen Actors Guild, governor of California

POLITICAL PARTY: Republican

ELECTED: 1980 and 1984

SERVED: January 1981 to January 1989

DIED: June 5, 2004, in Los Angeles, California, age ninety-three

PRESIDENTIAL TRIVIA:

★ Reagan was the first elected president to have been divorced. He was previously married from 1940 to 1949. He married the second time in 1952.

★ A former president of the Screen Actors Guild, Reagan was the first elected U.S. president who once led a labor union.

Ronald Wilson Reagan in 1981, the year he became president

CHAPTER EIGHT

CHEATING DEATH

"If I'd had this much attention in Hollywood, I'd have stayed there."
—RONALD REAGAN

THE ACTOR

ON MONDAY AFTERNOON, MARCH 30, 1981, RONALD REAGAN STEPPED from the shiny black presidential limousine at George Washington University Hospital in Washington, DC. He straightened his suit jacket and walked toward the doors of the emergency room with two Secret Service agents beside him.

As soon as Reagan stepped inside, he spotted a nurse approaching him. "I feel like I can't catch my breath," he told her.

Then he collapsed.

The Secret Service agents caught him before he hit the floor. With help from the nurse and a paramedic, they carried him onto a stretcher in the trauma section of the ER. The color had drained from his face. He struggled to get enough air.

Underneath his brand-new, pinstriped suit and monogrammed shirt, Ronald Reagan was bleeding internally. The President of the United States was at death's doorstep, and no one realized it.

Ronald Reagan got his start in Illinois, the son of a salesman. During high school and college, he played several sports and acted in plays. A strong swimmer, Reagan paid for college by working as a lifeguard for seven summers. After graduating from Eureka College in Illinois with a degree in economics and sociology, he took jobs at Iowa radio stations as a sports announcer.

In 1937, while in Los Angeles covering baseball spring training for an Iowa radio station, Reagan went for a screen test. Warner Brothers film studio liked what they saw, and they hired the twenty-six-year-old as an actor. His movie and television career lasted nearly thirty years, during which he acted in more than four dozen films. Throughout World War II, he helped make training films for the U.S. Army Air Corps.

Reagan had been his college's student body president. After the war, he became active in politics again. In 1947, he was elected president of the Screen Actors Guild and served six one-year terms.

Reagan campaigned for Democrat Harry Truman in the 1948 presidential election. During the next four presidential races, he backed

Ronald Reagan, age four, with his parents and older brother

Republicans Dwight Eisenhower, Richard Nixon, and Barry Goldwater because he preferred their policies to those of the Democratic Party. As a Hollywood celebrity, Reagan brought attention to these candidates. Although he had begun his adult life in the Great Depression as a Democrat supporting Franklin Roosevelt, Reagan changed his voter registration to Republican in 1962. "I'm not so sure *I* changed as much as the parties changed," he said.

Reagan started out as a radio sports announcer before becoming an actor. He gave up his pipe when his brother developed cancer of the voice box, which is often caused by smoking.

Reagan with his second wife, Nancy, and their two children, Ron and Patti, in 1960. He also had two children, Maureen and Michael, with his first wife, actress Jane Wyman.

Soon he had his own political ambitions. Retiring from his entertainment career, Reagan ran for governor of California in 1966 as a Republican. He defeated his opponent by almost a million votes. Four years later, he was reelected.

Having served as governor for eight years, Reagan focused on the presidency. In 1976, he tried to win the Republican nomination and lost to the current president, Gerald Ford. Reagan's time came in 1980 when he beat ten other candidates for the Republican nomination and went on to challenge the sitting Democratic president, Jimmy Carter (1977–1981).

TOO OLD?

When Reagan announced that he would be running for president in 1980, his age became an issue. If he won, he would be the oldest president ever inaugurated, less than a month shy of his seventieth birthday. Reagan vowed to be open about his health, saying that had been his policy since his first days in government.

Twenty-five years earlier, President Dwight Eisenhower had changed the standard for being honest about presidential health. He instructed his press secretary and staff to tell the truth about it, and Eisenhower's medical problems were described in detail. Not all presidents since then had upheld this standard (see chapter seven), but Reagan said, "the public had a right to the information."

Despite his age, Reagan was healthy, especially compared to many previous presidents. Careful about his diet and exercise, he hadn't gained weight the way older men often do. Aware that his father had been an alcoholic, Reagan was cautious about drinking, too. He imbibed no more than an infrequent cocktail before dinner or a glass of wine with his meal.

Many of his generation smoked heavily, but Reagan never used cigarettes, in part because of his family's illnesses. His father smoked three packs of cigarettes a day and had several heart attacks before one killed him at age sixty. Reagan smoked a pipe for a while, though he never deeply inhaled the smoke. He gave it up when his cigarette-smoking brother developed cancer of the voice box.

During the 1980 campaign, Reagan allowed six of his doctors to answer questions from a *New York Times* reporter. These physicians stated that Reagan's most recent medical examination earlier in the year showed that he had no evidence of heart or circulation problems. The candidate's only ailments were hay fever and some hearing loss in both ears. The only drugs he took were daily vitamins and occasional allergy pills and shots. His doctors agreed: He was medically fit to perform a president's duties.

Reagan was sensitive to the possibility of mental decline because his mother had died at age eighty after being senile for several years. In his interview with the *Times* reporter, Reagan said that he'd expect his doctor to consider that during annual exams. He declared, "If I were President and had any feeling at all that my capabilities had been reduced before a second term came, I would walk away."

His primary doctor told the reporter that, so far, he hadn't given Reagan any mental tests. The physician explained that these tests weren't routinely done on a man of Reagan's age unless there were signs of a problem . . . and there hadn't been any.

In his campaign for president, Reagan promised to promote smaller government, to reduce regulations on businesses, and to lower taxes. His age apparently didn't worry voters. In the November election, he beat President Carter in a landslide.

A REAL-LIFE DRAMA

Throughout his long acting career, Ronald Reagan had appeared in many fictional dramas. On March 30, 1981, seventy days after taking office, he became the star of a real one.

That Monday afternoon he was scheduled to speak to a labor organization at the Washington Hilton Hotel. Waiting for him there was John Hinckley, Jr., age twenty-five. Hinckley was obsessed with a young movie star. He wanted to get her attention and impress her, and he thought he could do that by shooting a president. Like Charles Guiteau, who exactly one hundred years earlier set his sights on President Garfield,

Hinckley came to Washington determined to kill President Reagan. Like Guiteau, Hinckley read about his target's schedule in the newspaper.

On the sidewalk outside the Hilton, Hinckley joined a group of reporters and photographers standing behind a rope. His position was about 10 feet (3 m) from the president's path between the hotel exit and the waiting presidential limousine. Although Hinckley didn't have press credentials, no one stopped him.

By 2:25 p.m., Reagan had finished his speech. As the president and his entourage left the building, Hinckley raised his handgun. He had a clear shot. *Pop, pop, pop, pop, pop, pop.* Six bullets left his gun.

When Reagan heard the shots, he turned toward the sound. "What the hell's that?" he said. A witness noticed "the smile just sort of washed off his face."

Seconds before, Secret Service Agent Tim McCarthy had opened the door of the armored limousine for the president. At the first sounds of a gunshot, he moved his body between Reagan and the shooter and spread his arms out to shield the president.

Secret Service Agent Jerry Parr, walking beside the president, pushed him into the backseat of the limo and jumped on top of him. Another agent slammed the door behind them, and the limo sped from the scene.

Four men had been hit by Hinckley's bullets. Three fell to the sidewalk. Reagan's press secretary, James Brady, was shot in the head. His blood flowed onto the concrete. District of Columbia policeman Thomas Delahanty, shot in the neck, lay on his stomach. Agent McCarthy was struck in the chest.

The fourth victim didn't know he'd been hit.

Secret Service agents, police officers, and bystanders wrestled Hinckley to the ground. Within moments, the agents forced him into a police car. No one wanted a replay of the killing of Lee Harvey Oswald while he was in police custody after John Kennedy's 1963 assassination.

On March 30, 1981, shortly before 2:30 p.m., Ronald Reagan waves to the crowd outside the side entrance of the Hilton Hotel in Washington. Seconds later, John Hinckley, Jr., fired off six shots from the small group on the right of the photograph. Secret Service Agent Jerry Parr, second from left in the light raincoat, pushed the president into the waiting limo as soon as he heard the gunshots.

Besides Reagan, bullets struck Press Secretary James Brady (third from left, behind Reagan) who was shot in the head; he remained paralyzed until his death in August 2014. Secret Service Agent Tim McCarthy in the light blue suit (on the right facing Reagan) was shot in the chest; he fully recovered. Metropolitan police officer Thomas Delahanty (close to the crowd looking toward Reagan) was shot in back of the neck; he had permanent nerve damage.

Inside the presidential limousine, Agent Parr quickly felt Reagan's upper body and head, searching for a gunshot wound. When he didn't detect one, Parr directed the driver to the White House where the president would be secure. He knew Reagan could still be in danger if the shooting was part of a conspiracy.

Reagan was in excruciating pain. "Get off, I think you've broken one of my ribs," he snapped at Parr. The agent moved off the president.

As Reagan sat upright, he coughed and blood came from his mouth. It was bright red and foamy, a sign that it was from his lungs. Change of plans. Parr called up to the limo driver to head to George Washington University Hospital, the closest trauma center.

Reagan's handkerchief was soaked with blood. The pain was intense, and he couldn't breathe in enough air. But when the limo pulled up to the emergency room, he climbed out on his own and walked toward the entrance. He barely made it inside before his legs gave way, and he had to be carried to the ER's trauma bay.

Nurses immediately cut off the president's clothes. His new suit lay on the floor in tatters. They quickly scanned his body and didn't see any injuries. They wondered if he was having a heart attack.

"I feel so bad," he told the nurses.

Reagan's White House physician, Dr. Daniel Ruge, arrived. He'd been at the Hilton and seen what happened. Ruge reassured the president, but he kept out of the way while the ER team focused on Reagan. The doctor stayed close to answer questions about the president's blood type, normal blood pressure, allergies, and other relevant health matters.

Reagan's skin looked gray. His blood pressure was dangerously low. He was bleeding internally, losing so much blood that he was at risk of going into shock.

To counteract his blood loss, a medical technician hooked up Reagan's arm with intravenous lines that provided fluids and red blood cells. One of the trauma team doctors put an oxygen mask over Reagan's nose and mouth to help him breathe easier.

Another doctor listened to the president's chest with a stethoscope. The left lung wasn't working normally. When he lifted Reagan's left arm, he saw a slit with blood around it in the skin below the armpit. It was a bullet entry wound. There was no exit wound anywhere. The bullet was still inside the president's body.

By thumping Reagan's left chest, doctors knew that the area around his left lung was full of blood. One of them inserted a tube between the president's ribs into the area and attached it to a suction machine. Blood poured out.

An X-ray of Reagan's chest showed the bullet near his heart. Doctors couldn't tell what structures the bullet had hit and damaged. Surgeons would have to operate to stop the bleeding.

The president had been in the hospital less than half an hour. When Reagan's wife, Nancy, arrived from the White House, he pulled up his oxygen mask. "Honey, I forgot to duck," he told her.

Then he was wheeled into the operating room. Besides the hospital team, Dr. Ruge and several Secret Service agents followed.

With the surgeons gathered around him, Reagan looked up and said to one, "I hope you're a Republican."

Although he was a Democrat, the doctor replied, "Today, Mr. President, we're all Republicans."

For three hours, the surgical team worked on Reagan. Doctors traced the bullet's path in his chest, but they needed additional X-rays to find it in his left lung. The bullet was flat like a dime and difficult for the surgeon to feel. It had become deformed when it hit the side of the armored presidential limousine. Bouncing off, the flattened bullet sliced into Reagan's body. Before the surgeon sewed up the wound, the president lost about half his blood supply.

A ROSY PICTURE

A United States president had been shot, and reporters were asking questions. The White House and George Washington University Hospital agreed that only one person should give medical updates. They handed the role to the hospital's Dr. Dennis O'Leary. O'Leary, who wasn't treating Reagan himself, passed on to the press what the president's doctors told him.

After Reagan was moved to the recovery room that evening, O'Leary briefed reporters. Explaining the injury and operation, he announced that the president was in stable condition and awake.

A reporter asked how close to death Reagan had been. O'Leary replied that "he was never in any serious danger. The bullet was really not very close to any vital structure." Another reporter tried to narrow down the bullet's distance from the heart. O'Leary answered, "Probably several inches."

Reagan Wounded by Assailant's Bullet; Prognosis Is 'Excellent'; 3 Others Shot

The headline from the *Washington Post* on March 31, 1984, the day after the assassination attempt

The press shared the information they were given with the public, but some of it turned out to be misleading and inaccurate. The initial accounts about Reagan walking into the hospital without help led people to think he wasn't badly wounded. Two days later, newspapers reported that they had learned the president was coughing up blood and having trouble breathing when he arrived at the ER.

A few days after the shooting, O'Leary admitted to a reporter that he had made his press briefings "as upbeat as I could without damaging my credibility." He initially understated the amount of blood that Reagan lost. In fact, it was so much that the president had been at risk of going into shock. The bullet had come within 1 inch (2.54 cm) of Reagan's heart, not several inches. Although O'Leary claimed he misspoke because he didn't have complete information from Reagan's doctors, the effect was to lessen the severity of the president's injury in the public's mind. O'Leary insisted that "Mr. Reagan's life was not in danger."

That wasn't the view of the president's doctors. Some of them thought O'Leary, in an effort to reassure the country, was giving too rosy a picture of Reagan's condition. The head of the trauma team later said, "The loss of blood was so rapid that, in my opinion, a 15-minute delay in getting the President to the hospital could have made a big difference and might even have been fatal." When he first saw Reagan in the ER, he believed "he was close to dying."

The White House tried to paint a rosy picture, too. Aides shared Reagan's humorous quips before his surgery, including the ones about hoping the doctors were all Republicans and telling his wife he forgot to duck. He made more wisecracks after he awoke post-surgery: "If I'd had this much attention in Hollywood, I'd have stayed there." And "Can we rewrite this scene beginning at the time I left the hotel?" The intended message to the public was that the president couldn't be too seriously hurt if he was cracking jokes.

White House aides were eager to show Reagan quickly resuming his presidential duties. Three of them arrived in the intensive care unit early on the morning after the shooting with a dairy bill for Reagan to sign into law. The president had left surgery less than thirteen hours before. One aide later recalled, "There was no hurry to sign, but we were convinced the

public needed to see that the Reagan presidency would not be sidetracked because of John Hinckley Jr."

To reinforce the message that it was business as usual, Vice President George H. W. Bush and several White House assistants also visited the president that day.

Reagan's recovery didn't go as smoothly as it looked to the nation, however. Three nights after his surgery, he ran a fever, had chills, and felt ill. Doctors described this to reporters as "a mild 'setback.'" Based on that assessment, headlines continued to say the president was in good condition.

The physicians prescribed antibiotics, but the fever continued. They were worried that he had a lung infection. One of the doctors later said, "The President was a lot sicker than most people realize." The symptoms went on until a change in the prescribed antibiotic slowly cleared them up. Reagan didn't return to normal until a week after the post-surgery crisis began.

The president's older daughter, Maureen, visited her father in the middle of his relapse. She was alarmed by how pale and weak he looked. "He was as close to death's door as I'd ever care to see him," she remembered. "I don't think the White House press people . . . ever let on how serious the President's condition was; one look at him a week after the shooting and you'd know that this was no routine recuperation." She kept up the deception by telling reporters that he was "terrific," when she knew he wasn't.

Twelve days after the assassination attempt, the president was discharged from the hospital. The White House released photographs of

The White House released this photograph of the president and his wife on April 3, 1981, strolling a hospital hallway just days after his injury. As the first photo taken after Reagan was shot, it was designed to show that he was recovering well. The image was cropped to cut out a nurse standing to Reagan's left. She held a medical machine connected to a chest tube extending from under his robe. Nancy Reagan didn't want the world to see her husband as an invalid.

The president leaves George Washington University Hospital on April 11, 1981, twelve days after the assassination attempt, holding hands with First Lady Nancy Reagan and their daughter, Patti. The hospital staff gathered to say goodbye. Reagan wore a bulletproof vest under his sweater.

Reagan at his desk three days later. The images implied that the president was back to his usual routine. Actually, he could only work a couple of hours a day at most. For several weeks, he felt chest pain and needed an afternoon nap. Gradually, his strength returned. He held his first cabinet meeting less than a month after the shooting and addressed Congress a few days after that.

Six weeks after his brush with death, Reagan's doctors declared him fully recovered. His surgeon said that "his own strong constitution and condition," not typical for a seventy-year-old, helped him survive the physical ordeal.

Though the nation was relieved that Reagan had escaped assassination, people were left with an inaccurate impression of the president's close call.

AMENDMENT IGNORED

In the hours after the assassination attempt, the president wasn't capable of making decisions. Yet no one in the White House turned to the Twenty-Fifth Amendment. Vice President Bush was on Air Force Two, flying back to Washington from Texas. He arrived at the White House about the time President Reagan left the operating room.

Several of those involved in discussions that day later wrote about why they opted not to invoke the amendment. "It would have alarmed the American people and our allies," the deputy press secretary recalled in his memoir, "giving them reason to believe that the President was much more seriously wounded than he now appeared to be."

White House physician Ruge said in an interview eight years later that he wished he had brought up the amendment with the White House. Ruge knew that Reagan would be under anesthesia and in intensive care for many hours, unable to communicate with anyone in the event of a national emergency. He thought the vice president should have had executive power for a couple of days. The doctor admitted that he was so busy monitoring the president that he didn't think about the amendment until the middle of the night, after he was sure Reagan would live. He regretted not bringing it up when he briefed the cabinet the next morning.

Ronald Reagan was the first sitting president to survive an assassin's bullet. Four of his predecessors were less fortunate. Reagan's would-be assassin, John Hinckley, Jr., was found not guilty by reason of insanity and sent to a Washington mental institution. He was released in 2016. The insanity defense had not worked for President Garfield's assassin, Charles Guiteau. He was hanged.

In Reagan's memoirs, he confessed that he felt guilty for accusing Secret Service Agent Parr of breaking his rib. The president realized that

Reagan owned a ranch in California where he cut firewood, fixed fences, and cleared brush. He rides his horse there in August 1981, five months after the assassination attempt.

Parr had protected him by jumping on his back and then saved his life by heading to the hospital. He was grateful to both Parr and Agent McCarthy for putting their lives on the line for him. Tim McCarthy is the only Secret Service agent to take a bullet for a president.

Reagan's near-death experience deepened his religious faith. He wrote in his diary the day he returned to the White House from the hospital, "Whatever happens now I owe my life to God and will try to serve him in every way I can."

COLON TROUBLE

Reagan ran for reelection in 1984 when he was seventy-three. Once again, concerns about his age arose.

In the first televised debate against his Democratic opponent, Walter Mondale, Reagan performed poorly. As a former actor, he'd proven over the years that he knew how to deliver an effective speech. But in the debate, he rambled and seemed confused. Afterward, commentators questioned whether he was too old to serve another term. Reagan's aides claimed that he'd been tired. Still, the president remained far ahead of Mondale in the polls of likely voters.

Two weeks later, in the second debate, Reagan met the criticism head-on . . . with a joke. When the moderator asked about his age being a problem, Reagan replied with his trademark smile, "I will not make age an issue of this campaign. I am not going to exploit, for political purposes, my opponent's youth and inexperience." Mondale was fifty-six. Everyone laughed, including Mondale. Reagan won reelection in a landslide, taking forty-nine of fifty states.

Six months into his second term, Reagan's health again made headlines. In March 1985, during a regular examination of his colon, doctors spotted a small polyp. These growths are usually harmless, but they can develop into cancer. On Friday, July 12, Reagan was admitted to the Bethesda Naval Hospital to remove it.

In the routine procedure, the surgeons spotted a second growth in Reagan's colon. It was bigger than the first one, with a diameter of about 2 inches (5 cm), and it looked cancerous. Getting it out required major surgery. With approval from Reagan and his wife, the doctors decided to operate the next day.

After the assassination attempt, the White House had learned that the press gained access to Reagan's emergency room medical records at George Washington University Hospital. Determined to avoid that this time, Nancy Reagan was against allowing the surgeons to discuss details with reporters. Her husband deserved some privacy, even if he was the president.

Nancy told the White House spokesman, Larry Speakes, not to say the alarming words "cancer" or "malignant" when he announced the president's operation. Speakes used the word "polyp" instead.

On the morning of his surgery, Reagan signed a letter to the speaker of the House of Representatives and the president pro tempore of the Senate, who were next in succession after the vice president. The letter stated that he was temporarily handing over authority to Vice President Bush. Reagan wrote that he did not want to set a precedent by officially invoking the Twenty-Fifth Amendment because he didn't think the situation was what the amendment's drafters meant.

During the surgery, doctors removed the large polyp and part of the president's colon. Bush had presidential authority while Reagan was drugged and asleep for nearly eight hours.

Nancy lost her battle to silence the surgeons, who met with the press alongside Speakes and explained that the growth was cancerous. But because the cancer hadn't spread, they said that Reagan needed no further treatment, such as radiation or chemicals.

Throughout the following days, Speakes was cagey about details of the president's recovery, giving only positive remarks and avoiding any specifics when reporters asked for them.

On July 27, two weeks after his surgery, Reagan taped an interview about his health. He made a point of declaring, "I had cancer. I don't have it anymore, and I feel fine." Although his remark reflected his optimistic view of life, it also helped to dispel any public concern that he was ill.

The president's colon was closely monitored going forward. In 1987, two years after his operation, doctors found and removed several more polyps during his regular colonoscopy. The growths were harmless.

The first photograph taken on July 14, 1985, the day after President Reagan's colon cancer surgery. Years later, the White House spokesman revealed that the photo was carefully shot to hide the tube Reagan had in his nose.

KEEP IT QUIET

Less than three weeks after his colon cancer surgery, reporters noticed a bandage on the president's nose. When they asked Speakes about it, he said that a dermatologist, whom he refused to name, had removed a small piece of skin. Reporters asked whether the skin was being tested for cancer. Speakes replied that no additional treatment was necessary.

Actually, the president's current White House physician, Dr. Burton Smith, suspected that the spot was cancer. Smith sent the skin sample to a lab for testing under a false name.

Nancy Reagan didn't want the media to connect this with her husband's colon cancer. She feared there would be speculation that his cancer was spreading. She asked Dr. Smith to call the spot a pimple when talking to the press. He did.

Mrs. Reagan also pressured Speakes not to reveal the truth. With her approval, he put out a statement saying that the spot was irritation from tape that held a nasal tube during the president's hospital stay. When reporters asked for more details, he was evasive.

The press was irked that Speakes wasn't telling them why Reagan had minor surgery, what tests were done, and what the results were. They kept asking questions. Was there an infection? Did the president have cancer?

The truth finally emerged a few days later from the president himself. Reagan told a group of reporters that the tests had come back showing he had a form of skin cancer caused by sun exposure. Having such a common type of cancer, he said, did not mean he was prone to cancer. Now that the spot was removed, he required no more treatment.

To the reporters, it seemed as if the White House had intentionally limited information. Reagan denied that.

Nancy Reagan resented the way the press made a fuss over the minor problem. "Sometimes you wonder if they *want* you to be sick," she complained.

About a year later, Reagan learned that he needed surgery again. His prostate gland was enlarged, interfering with urination. The operation was considered uncomplicated, and it was scheduled for early January 1987. The White House publicized the surgery date three weeks ahead so that no one would think that it was an emergency.

Nancy Reagan felt that the operation's details were too personal to share with the world. Rather than rely on government surgeons like those who had performed Reagan's 1984 colon cancer surgery, she brought in a team of doctors she knew from the Mayo Clinic in Minnesota.

Because the president had local anesthesia and was awake during the surgery, the White House didn't pass his duties to the vice president.

After the procedure, Reagan's White House physician announced that the routine surgery was over in an hour and there had been no signs of cancer. Before the press could directly question the Mayo Clinic surgeons, they had left Washington for home.

THE END OF THE TRAIL

In January 1989, with his two terms over, Ronald Reagan headed for his California home. Vice President George H. W. Bush had been elected president (1989–1993).

When Reagan was on vacation in Mexico in July 1989, his horse threw him 15 feet (about 4.6 m) in the air. Upon landing, he hit his head and was briefly knocked unconscious. A medical examination revealed blood between his skull and brain, a condition that can put pressure on the brain. Since Reagan didn't have any lasting problems like headaches or dizziness, his doctor didn't think further treatment was required.

While flying to Minnesota in September for his annual physical at the Mayo Clinic, Reagan bumped his head on an overhead bin. During his exam, the Mayo doctors detected an expanding area of bleeding around his brain. Whether it was from his fall two months before or from hitting his head in the plane, they decided Reagan needed surgery to drain the fluid. The operation was successful, and the former president returned to California a week later.

After the surgery, Reagan's doctors gave him rigorous annual tests to assess his brain's health. Nothing raised alarms until the summer of 1993. The doctors conducted more testing to confirm their suspicions.

In November 1994, Reagan released a handwritten letter addressed to "My Fellow Americans." He revealed that he had been diagnosed with the early stage of Alzheimer's disease, an incurable brain illness that gradually erases memory and eventually leads to death. In his two-page letter, Reagan thanked the public for the "honor of allowing me to serve as your President." He wrote, "I now begin the journey that will lead me into the sunset of my life. I know that for America there will always be a bright dawn ahead."

Reagan stepped out of the limelight after his diagnosis.

Ten years later, in June 2004, Ronald Reagan died at his California home of pneumonia, a common cause of death in Alzheimer's disease patients. He was ninety-three.

Reagan reveals: I have Alzheimer's

Reagan faces fight of his life

Media across the country and world reported on Reagan's Alzheimer's disease diagnosis. These headlines are from the *Chicago Tribune* (top) and the *Baltimore Sun* (bottom) on November 6, 1994. Alzheimer's experts praised Reagan for going public and raising awareness of the ailment. At the time, about 4 million Americans suffered from it. Today the number is nearly 7 million.

Various observers later suggested that Reagan had early signs of Alzheimer's disease while he was in the White House. This is doubtful, however. On average, Alzheimer's patients survive from seven to ten years after their diagnosis. Reagan had been out of office for fifteen years when he died. Starting with his head injury in 1989 and continuing for the next few years, doctors carefully tested his brain. Everything was normal throughout that period.

Five presidents pose at the opening of the Ronald Reagan Presidential Library in California on November 4, 1991. From left to right: Gerald Ford (1974–1977), Richard Nixon (1969–1974), George H. W. Bush (1989–1993), Reagan (1981–1989), Jimmy Carter (1977–1981).

A more likely explanation for his behavior was his management style. He typically left details to his aides unless he was involved in an issue important to him. This sometimes created problems during his presidency and made him appear forgetful and distracted.

Ronald Reagan entered office as the oldest president yet. He survived a gunshot wound and had several surgeries during his eight years in office, successfully recovering each time. He had pledged "to divulge accurate and timely information" about his health. But when his medical condition differed from the way the White House wanted to portray Reagan, people around him—aides, family, doctors—protected his image with deception.

SURVIVED THE PRESIDENCY

JOSEPH BIDEN

46th PRESIDENT

BORN: November 20, 1942, in Scranton, Pennsylvania

PROFESSION BEFORE PRESIDENCY: lawyer, U.S. senator from Delaware, U.S. vice president

POLITICAL PARTY: Democrat

ELECTED: 2020

SERVED: January 2021 to January 2025

DIED: still living

PRESIDENTIAL TRIVIA:

★ When Biden was sworn in as a U.S. senator at age thirty years, forty-four days, he was one of the youngest in history to hold the office. The U.S. Constitution sets thirty as a senator's minimum age.

★ When Biden took the presidential oath at age seventy-eight, he was the oldest to ever hold that office. The next oldest was Ronald Reagan, who left office at age seventy-seven.

Joseph Robinette Biden, Jr., in 2021, the year he became president

CHAPTER NINE
THE DISASTROUS DEBATE

"No one's pushing me out. I'm not leaving."
—JOSEPH BIDEN

THE CHALLENGE

AFTER A LONG CAREER AS A SENATOR AND VICE PRESIDENT, DEMOCRAT Joe Biden was elected president in November 2020, beating the sitting president, Donald Trump (2017–2021, 2025–). During the campaign, Biden talked as if he intended to serve a single term. He changed his mind. On April 25, 2023, more than two years after taking office, Biden released a three-minute video to launch his bid for reelection. His slogan: "Let's finish this job."

Although he had a few opponents in the 2024 Democratic primaries, Biden won enough of his party's votes to secure the nomination. By early March 2024, former President Trump had won the Republican primaries to become his party's candidate. The race between the two major parties was set.

During the primary season, Trump repeatedly challenged Biden to a one-on-one debate. News organizations pushed for it, too. At first, the Biden campaign avoided committing to a debate. But in mid-May 2024, Biden announced on social media that he was willing. In a video, he taunted Trump: "Make my day, pal."

Surveys of likely voters showed a close race between the two men. Some observers speculated that Biden's campaign agreed to the debate to get more media attention as soon as possible. Political analysts suggested that eighty-one-year-old Biden needed to put to rest the concerns that he was too old. A debate was a way for him to contrast himself with Trump, who was just three and a half years younger.

Biden had performed well in his March 2024 State of the Union Address. In 2020, the majority of viewers said he outmatched Trump in their two debates. President Biden's team thought he could do it again.

The campaigns agreed on dates for a pair of debates. Only one ever took place.

THE BOY FROM SCRANTON

Joe Biden's journey to the White House began in Scranton, Pennsylvania. Born there in 1942, he was the oldest of four children. When he was a boy, his family moved to Delaware where his father found work as a salesman. After graduating from the University of Delaware, Joe attended law school at Syracuse University in New York. Then he returned to his home state to practice law and enter politics.

In 1972, Biden ran for the U.S. Senate. He wasn't expected to win. His Republican opponent had been Delaware's senator for twelve years, and the only political office Biden had ever held was on a county council. Besides, Biden was barely the minimum age for a senator set by the U.S.

Joe Biden's first official U.S. Senate photograph, 1973

Constitution. The election was close, but Biden won.

Six weeks later, his excitement about the victory changed to grief. On December 18, Biden's wife, Neilia, was out Christmas shopping. The Bidens' three young children were with her in the family station wagon. As she drove through an intersection, a truck hit her vehicle. Neilia and one-year-old Naomi were killed. Beau and Hunter, ages four and three, were badly injured but survived. Biden took his Senate oath of office in his sons' hospital room two weeks after the accident.

Biden spent thirty-six years in the U.S. Senate and twice ran for the Democratic presidential nomination. He announced his first try in the spring of 1987 ahead of the 1988 general election. But he was forced to drop out of the Democratic Party's primary race after three months when he was accused of plagiarizing other politicians' speeches. Later revelations disclosed that in law school he had copied a published article without citing the source. Biden had also lied about his law school class rank.

Five years after his first wife died, Biden remarried. He and his second wife, Jill (above), have one daughter, Ashley.

Senator Biden ran again in 2008. He quit the primary race after his poor showing in the Iowa caucuses. Later that year, Senator Barack Obama became the Democrats' nominee and asked Biden to join the ticket as vice president. The Obama–Biden team won the 2008 general election and was reelected in 2012.

After eight years as vice president, Biden ran for

Barack Obama (2009–2017) and Joe Biden in August 2008 during the presidential campaign

president a third time in the 2020 race at age seventy-seven. Because his age and health were issues for voters, his primary care doctor, Kevin O'Connor, released Biden's medical report to prove that he was capable of the job. O'Connor, an army doctor, had been assigned as Biden's physician during his vice presidency. After Biden left that office, O'Connor retired from the military and continued as his private doctor.

O'Connor's December 2019 report included Biden's surgeries for two brain aneurysms in 1988. Since then, he'd had no other aneurysms. He'd also had surgeries to repair orthopedic and sports injuries, to open up his sinuses, and to remove his gallbladder. Biden didn't smoke or drink alcohol. He did take medications to lower his cholesterol, prevent blood clots, and relieve seasonal allergies. Dr. O'Connor concluded the summary by calling Biden a "healthy, vigorous, 77-year-old male, who is fit to successfully execute the duties of the Presidency."

Biden ultimately received the Democrats' nomination.

The 2020 presidential campaign took place during the COVID-19 pandemic, and there were fewer political rallies and in-person appearances than in typical elections. Throughout the campaign, Trump charged that Biden suffered from cognitive decline and had taken performance-enhancing drugs during the primaries. Trump presented no proof to back up his claim.

On November 3, 2020, Biden won the general election. When he took office in January 2021, he made Dr. O'Connor his official White House physician.

Biden takes the presidential oath of office, January 20, 2021.

Three presidents at the January 2017 inauguration of Donald Trump: (left to right) Barack Obama, Joe Biden, Donald Trump. The fourth man next to Biden is Senator Chuck Schumer of New York.

THE OLDEST PRESIDENT

Soon after Biden became president, concerns about his age resurfaced. In March 2021, the seventy-eight-year-old mistakenly referred to his vice president, Kamala Harris, as "President Harris." He didn't correct himself. The next day, he tripped three times as he climbed the steps of Air Force One. The White House dismissed the falls as "nothing more than a misstep on the stairs." Then in June 2021, at a news conference during an international meeting in England, the president mixed up the countries of Libya and Syria several times.

In the 1930s and 40s, Franklin Roosevelt's White House team was able to prevent the press from photographing him in a wheelchair. Hiding a twenty-first-century president was more difficult. On various media, the public saw the president shuffling and tripping. Occasionally while reading his teleprompter during a speech, he misspoke the words, apparently not realizing it. When speaking without a teleprompter, Biden at times lost his train of thought midsentence.

Since these public blunders drew attention to Biden's age, the White House made efforts to avoid repeats. The president began wearing black dress sneakers with rubber soles to keep him more sure-footed. He climbed onto the presidential plane using a staircase that was less steep than usual so that he didn't trip.

Biden held fewer press conferences and interviews than recent presidents. His political critics pointed to this as evidence that the White House shielded him from unscripted appearances because he wasn't physically and mentally up to the demands of the presidency.

The White House claimed that Biden's health was fine, presenting reports of Dr. O'Connor's annual physical exams to confirm it. In the 2023 medical report, O'Connor wrote that Biden had been examined by specialists from various medical fields, including heart, spine, feet, and nervous system. He described the president as fit and healthy, with no nerve disorders. His stiff gait was from arthritis in his spine and feet.

The public wasn't reassured. An April 2023 *NBC News* survey showed that seven in ten American adults were against Biden serving another term. Nearly half of those people said it was because of his age. An Associated Press poll of only Democrats found that less than half wanted him to be their party's candidate again.

Nevertheless, on April 25, 2023, President Biden announced that he was running for reelection.

He would be challenged by several other Democrats. Among them was Robert Kennedy, Jr., who also entered the race in April 2023. He was the nephew of President John Kennedy and son of Robert Kennedy, a presidential candidate who was assassinated during the 1968 Democratic primaries. The younger Kennedy charged "that President Biden suffered from a degenerative condition that was not going to improve and that it would make it impossible for him to govern effectively."

On June 1, 2023, President Joe Biden tripped over a sandbag and fell onstage at the U.S. Air Force Academy graduation. Though uninjured, he had to be helped up. Videos and photographs of the tumble appeared on major news broadcasts, in newspapers, and online.

In October 2023, Democratic Congressman Dean Phillips of Minnesota launched his bid for the presidential nomination. During his campaign, he argued that Biden's age and infirmity made it unlikely he could win again, saying, "He's in decline."

The issue of age arose on the Republican side, too. In February 2023, former South Carolina governor and United Nations ambassador Nikki Haley announced that she was running for the 2024 Republican presidential nomination. Throughout her yearlong campaign, she called for mental competency tests for any candidate older than seventy-five. That included both Trump and Biden. She said that politicians should prove to voters that their thinking was still keen and astute enough to handle important responsibilities.

When Trump was president in 2018, he took such a test as part of his annual physical. During the 2020 presidential race, Biden declared that there was no reason for him to do so. He told a CBS reporter in August 2020, "No, I haven't taken a test. Why the hell would I take a test?"

DAMAGING REPORTS

By the beginning of 2024, whispers about the president's health had grown louder around Washington. Biden reportedly had days when he was alert and seemed normal. On bad days, however, he appeared very different.

A few lawmakers who met with him thought he sometimes was disoriented, even closing his eyes during conversations as if he had zoned out. They noticed that he forgot details that should have been familiar to him.

At one fundraiser, Biden repeated the same story twice. During a televised White House event in January, the president confused the names of two cabinet secretaries who both had Hispanic names. He called out the name of one of them who wasn't even in the room.

His mistakes also involved world leaders. At two campaign fundraisers in early February 2024, President Biden twice mixed up the current German chancellor with her predecessor who died seven years before. At another event the same week, he confused the name of the French president with the one who had died in 1996.

Biden's aides and allies were quick to dismiss these incidents. They said that the president's mind was sharp and his memory of events and information was good. But an official Justice Department report contradicted this.

In January 2023, the attorney general had appointed a special counsel, Robert Hur. Hur was to investigate the discovery of classified government documents at Biden's former Washington office and Delaware home. The materials had been there for several years after Biden left the vice presidency in January 2017 and became a private citizen. As part of Hur's investigation, he interviewed the president on two days in October 2023.

On February 5, 2024, Hur submitted his final report to the attorney general, and it was made public a few days later. In the report, the special counsel wrote that he found evidence of Biden mishandling the documents. Additionally, Hur said that during Biden's October interview, the president had trouble remembering when he had been vice president and when one of his adult sons had died of cancer.

The report referred to Biden's "diminished faculties in advancing age." It characterized him as "a sympathetic, well-meaning elderly man with a poor memory." Hur determined that this would make it hard to get a jury to convict Biden of any crimes. Therefore, the president would not be charged.

Hur's report rekindled questions about Biden's mental acuity. The president's allies argued that the report misrepresented his statements during the interviews.

Biden's political opponents said that this news showed that he wasn't fit to be commander in chief. Several Republicans in Congress called for the vice president and cabinet to invoke Section 4 of the Twenty-Fifth Amendment and remove Biden from office.

At the White House a few hours after the report's release, Biden responded to it. He testily told the press, "I'm well-meaning, and I'm an elderly man—and I know what the hell I'm doing. . . . I'm the most qualified person in this country to be president of the United States and finish the job I started." Yet in the same press conference, he misidentified the leader of Egypt as the president of Mexico.

Three weeks later, Dr. O'Connor released the results of the president's 2024 annual physical. It didn't indicate any major changes in Biden's health since the year before. O'Connor's conclusion: "He continues to be fit for duty."

Reporters wanted to ask Dr. O'Connor questions in person, but the White House did not make him available. They asked Press Secretary Karine Jean-Pierre why the president's physical did not include a cognitive test, especially in light of the special counsel's report.

She replied, "He passes a cognitive test every day, every day as he moves from one topic to another topic, understanding the granular level of these topics." She went on, "The president doesn't need a cognitive test. The doctor doesn't believe he needs one."

In almost all opinion polls, the majority of likely voters disagreed. The public saw the president on their screens. They noticed his stiff gait and occasional stumbles. They heard his slurred speech and verbal slipups. Many thought his mental and physical abilities were declining before their eyes. They wondered what he'd be like at the end of a second term at age eighty-six.

Congressman Dean Phillips warned his party, "Shame on all of you pretending everything is ok. You are leading us—and him—into a disaster, and you damn well know it." Phillips was criticized by the Democratic leadership for his comments. He didn't get enough votes in the states' primary elections to beat President Biden for the nomination, and he dropped out of the race in early March 2024.

Robert Kennedy, Jr., alleged that the Democratic National Committee protected Biden by changing the primary rules and shielding him from debates with his Democratic challengers. Kennedy withdrew from the Democratic primaries in October 2023 to run as an independent candidate. He later suspended his campaign in August 2024 to support former President Trump, charging that the Democrats "ran a sham primary."

Despite all of this, by March 12, 2024, Biden had amassed enough votes in the Democratic primaries to clinch his nomination for reelection.

AN UNFORTUNATE JUNE

On June 4, the *Wall Street Journal* published accounts of the president's physical and mental decline. The article was based on interviews with several dozen people—both Republicans and Democrats—who had had contact with Biden during the previous year.

The White House condemned the newspaper's exposé, saying that unflattering reports about Biden's performance were false, partisan attacks. The president's mind was sharp, they said. He was engaged and decisive. The press office pointed to Biden's February physical exam. Neither Dr. O'Connor nor the specialists he consulted thought that the president needed a cognitive test.

But several incidents caught on video seemed to dispute that. At a June 10 White House celebration of Juneteenth, Biden came across as wooden and uninvolved while others danced to music. Some witnesses later said that the president's garbled speech and awkward behavior concerned them. At a

June 15 Hollywood fundraiser, Biden looked frail and befuddled. At one point, former President Barack Obama took his arm and appeared to lead him off the stage.

White House Press Secretary Jean-Pierre accused the media of distorting these episodes by editing and cropping the videos. She called them "cheap fakes videos." The Biden team maintained that the president's mental acuity was as good as ever.

At 9 p.m. Thursday, June 27, President Biden and former President Trump

Donald Trump (left) and Joe Biden during the June 27, 2024, debate. Biden's performance that night was pivotal in his reelection quest.

took the stage at CNN's Atlanta, Georgia, studios for their ninety-minute debate. They did not make eye contact or shake hands as is customary before a debate. Several broadcast and streaming networks carried the debate, and about 51 million people tuned in.

From the first few minutes, it was obvious that something was amiss with President Biden. His voice was raspy. He slurred his words. His sentences trailed away unfinished. His answers to the moderators' questions veered off topic, and some were incoherent. Biden didn't seem able to think on his feet when responding to follow-up questions or challenges from Trump. The split screen of the two men often showed the president staring glassy-eyed with his mouth hanging open while Trump spoke.

Many viewers were shocked and alarmed. They had believed the Biden team's insistence that the president was fit to serve for another four years. The debate raised doubts about that and about his ability to win in November.

Republicans proclaimed that President Biden's performance proved what they had been saying ever since the president took office: He was physically and mentally deteriorating.

The post-debate headlines were devastating. "Biden's Biggest Weakness—His Age—on Full Display at Debate"; "Inside Biden's Debate Disaster and the Scramble to Quell Democratic Panic"; "Biden's Disastrous Debate Pitches His Reelection Bid into Crisis." Media stories described Biden as confused and "struggling to string thoughts together."

News outlets that were usually supportive of the president ran editorials calling for him to end his reelection campaign. The *New York Times* editorial board wrote that Biden failed to prove that he could handle another term in office, or that he could beat Donald Trump in the election. The newspaper said, "More than once, he struggled to make it to the end of a sentence."

PUSHING BACK

The day after the debate, President Biden attended a campaign rally in North Carolina. He admitted to the crowd that he wasn't young anymore. He knew that he no longer walked, talked, or debated the way he used to. But he made clear he did not plan to leave the race. "When you get knocked down, you get back up," he said.

The White House declared that the president's debate performance was atypical. His aides blamed the president's hoarse voice and shaky performance on a cold and jet lag from his international trips. Critics noted that those travels had ended nearly two weeks earlier.

One of Biden's advisors said, "It [the debate] doesn't reflect the experience I have with him on a daily basis." Another advisor stated, "He's inquisitive. Focused. He remembers. He's sharp."

Those claims didn't erase what tens of millions of Americans had seen on the debate stage in live, unedited video. In a Pew Research poll taken the week after the debate, just 24 percent of registered voters said the phrase "mentally sharp" described President Biden very or fairly well. This was in contrast to 58 percent who described Trump that way. Attitudes about Biden's cognition had changed drastically since he ran for office in October 2020. At that time, the Pew survey found 46 percent of registered voters described him as mentally sharp.

A few Democrats urged Biden to drop out of the race. Gradually, other voices joined the chorus. Congressional representatives and senators who were in close reelection contests were worried that a poor showing by Biden on Election Day would hurt their chances.

Biden fought back, trying to reassure Democrats, campaign donors, and voters that he should remain the party's nominee. On a Zoom call, he insisted, "No one's pushing me out. I'm not leaving."

Headlines after the debate as Biden pushes back against critics, from the *Wall Street Journal*, July 9, 2024 (top), and *Politico*, July 3, 2024 (bottom)

President Digs In, Reiterates He Won't Quit Race

Biden tells party lawmakers that voters selected him as their nominee

Biden: 'No one's pushing me out'

News articles began quoting people (on and off the record) who admitted that Biden's debate performance resembled off-camera moments they had witnessed for more than a year. The president, they reported, was sometimes bewildered or briefly froze. Several media outlets accused the White House press office of trying to shut down stories about Biden's age and mental acuity.

At a White House press briefing, reporters asked to question Dr. Kevin O'Connor directly and to see more of Biden's medical records. Was the president being treated for a neurological disease?

Press Secretary Jean-Pierre refused to provide any details, citing medical privacy. By law, a person's health records can't be accessed unless the patient gives permission. A president is not required to release those records.

To calm the uproar, O'Connor issued a memo on July 8, repeating what he'd written after Biden's February physical. The president did not suffer from a neurological disorder, including stroke or Parkinson's disease (which can cause stiffness, shuffling, and slurred speech). The memo didn't mention a cognitive test, nor did O'Connor make himself available to the press.

On July 11, an embarrassing incident at a meeting of NATO allies in Washington raised more questions about the president's mental fitness. Biden mixed up the name of Ukrainian President Volodymyr Zelenskyy with Russian President Vladimir Putin, the man who had sent troops to invade Ukraine more than two years earlier. People in the room gasped. A president of the United States was not expected to confuse the names of the leaders in a major international conflict. Yet Biden had done it again.

Later that evening, President Biden held a solo press conference. It was the first one he'd had since November 2023, nearly eight months earlier. His supporters hoped that a successful performance dealing with reporters would counteract the debate debacle. Despite a few mistakes, including referring to "Vice President Trump" instead of his vice president, Kamala Harris, Biden appeared more forceful and cogent.

One reporter asked the president if he'd be willing to take cognitive tests or another physical to verify that he had no neurological problems. Biden replied that he would if his doctors thought he should. "I'll do it," he said. "But no one is suggesting that to me now."

PARTY REVOLT

In October 1984, Ronald Reagan had also performed poorly in a presidential debate. But he was far ahead of his opponent in the polls, and the Republican Party stuck with him. In the next debate, Reagan bounced back. Things were much different for Joe Biden.

Behind the scenes, his support was crumbling. Three key Democratic leaders—the Senate majority leader, the House of Representatives minority leader, and the former speaker of the House—separately spoke with the president. They informed him that congressional Democrats were

Biden meets with Ukraine's President Volodymyr Zelenskyy at the White House, December 12, 2023. The United States supplied Ukraine with weapons and military equipment after Russia's February 2022 invasion of the country.

anxious that he would lose the election and take them down with him. The party might lose not only the presidency but also both chambers of Congress.

Biden was adamant about staying in the race. He didn't believe polls that showed he would likely lose to his opponent. In fact, he was sure he was the best candidate the party had.

On Saturday, July 13, startling news took over the headlines. In Butler, Pennsylvania, at a campaign rally for former President Donald Trump, a would-be assassin shot and slightly wounded Trump's ear. The shooter killed a spectator and seriously wounded two others before a Secret Service sniper killed him on his rooftop perch.

Minutes after being shot, a bloody Trump raised his fist to assure rally attendees that he had survived the assassination attempt. The photograph of the moment energized his supporters and provided a stark contrast to the frail-looking Biden millions had seen during the debate.

Within two days of the shooting, Biden was again sitting for media interviews and making public appearances to demonstrate that he was able to win reelection.

Things didn't go according to plan.

On Wednesday, July 17, while the president was campaigning in Las Vegas, he tested positive for COVID-19. It was the third time he'd had the virus in two years. Dr. O'Connor released a memo saying that Biden had begun taking the antiviral drug Paxlovid and would fly to his home in Delaware to recover.

News video showed the president straining to climb the steps onto Air Force One in Nevada, appearing weak and feeble. It was not the image of a strong president that his campaign had been trying to project.

The White House informed the press that Biden would return to campaigning the following week, after he had recuperated. The president, his family, and his closest advisers still believed he could beat Trump, citing the times in his life when he had surprised doubters.

But on Saturday evening, July 20, a discussion with his two closest aides shifted Biden's thinking. They presented evidence that three weeks of unrelenting opposition to his candidacy made it impossible to stay in the race. Biden had lost support from Democratic Party leaders and lawmakers. Donors were withholding their money. The campaign's own opinion polls indicated that voters didn't want him to run. It seemed clear that he wouldn't win the election.

On Sunday afternoon, July 21, Biden announced on social media that he was ending his campaign for reelection. In his statement, he wrote that he made the decision "in the best interest of my party and the country." Biden endorsed Vice President Harris as the Democratic Party's presidential nominee.

Biden makes stunning decision to pull out of 2024 race

Headlines in reaction to Biden's decision not to run for reelection, from the *Washington Post*, July 21, 2024 (top), and the *Wall Street Journal*, July 22, 2024 (bottom)

Biden Drops Out, Endorses Harris

JOSEPH R. BIDEN, JR.

July 21, 2024

My Fellow Americans,

Over the past three and a half years, we have made great progress as a Nation.

Today, America has the strongest economy in the world. We've made historic investments in rebuilding our Nation, in lowering prescription drug costs for seniors, and in expanding affordable health care to a record number of Americans. We've provided critically needed care to a million veterans exposed to toxic substances. Passed the first gun safety law in 30 years. Appointed the first African American woman to the Supreme Court. And passed the most significant climate legislation in the history of the world. America has never been better positioned to lead than we are today.

I know none of this could have been done without you, the American people. Together, we overcame a once in a century pandemic and the worst economic crisis since the Great Depression. We've protected and preserved our Democracy. And we've revitalized and strengthened our alliances around the world.

It has been the greatest honor of my life to serve as your President. And while it has been my intention to seek reelection, I believe it is in the best interest of my party and the country for me to stand down and to focus solely on fulfilling my duties as President for the remainder of my term.

I will speak to the Nation later this week in more detail about my decision.

For now, let me express my deepest gratitude to all those who have worked so hard to see me reelected. I want to thank Vice President Kamala Harris for being an extraordinary partner in all this work. And let me express my heartfelt appreciation to the American people for the faith and trust you have placed in me.

I believe today what I always have: that there is nothing America can't do – when we do it together. We just have to remember we are the United States of America.

Joe Biden

Immediately, the public and press speculated about his sudden turnaround. Some news accounts reported that Biden had been bullied out of office by fellow Democrats because his cognitive decline had become too difficult to deny. The Republican Speaker of the House of Representatives Mike Johnson called it "the largest political coverup in U.S. history."

Johnson wasn't alone in suspecting a cover-up. A YouGov poll of registered voters conducted during the two days following Biden's announcement found that 54 percent were certain there had been a cover-up of his health. (Another 16 percent weren't sure.) They blamed his family, White House staff, Democrats in Congress, Vice President Harris, and the news media for concealing the truth.

At a press briefing three days after Biden left the race, reporters asked Jean-Pierre why the president had changed his mind so abruptly after weeks of vowing to stay in the race. Was it his health? Had there been a cover-up?

The press secretary responded, "There's been no cover-up. I want to be very clear about that. . . . It has nothing to do with his health." When pushed, she said that the president would speak for himself in his televised statement that evening.

President Biden didn't answer those questions in his Oval Office address.

But three weeks later, during an interview with *CBS News*, he said, "A number of my Democratic colleagues in the House and Senate thought that I was gonna hurt them in the races. And I was concerned if I stayed in the race, that would be the topic." He went on to say, "I had a really, really bad day in that debate because I was sick. But I have no serious problem."

Biden's letter announcing that he was dropping out of the presidential race

Some observers saw the situation differently. In late August, the editorial board of the *Washington Post* acknowledged that the June 4 *Wall Street Journal* exposé had been correct. Biden "had shown signs of slipping for a long time, but his inner circle worked to conceal his decline."

On the eve of the August Democratic Party convention, a *New York Times* columnist wrote, "A coterie of powerful Democrats maneuvered behind the scenes to push an incumbent president out of the race."

In 1884, President Chester Arthur, secretly knowing that he suffered from an incurable disease, opted not to run for reelection. In 1920, Democratic Party leaders worked together to keep a diminished Woodrow Wilson from seeking a third term after his debilitating stroke. In the summer of 1944, the visibly ailing Franklin Roosevelt prepared to run for his fourth term. The Democratic Party leadership discreetly arranged for a vice presidential nominee they could work with in case the president died. Their choice, Senator Harry Truman, ended up assuming the presidency less than three months after Roosevelt's fourth inauguration.

And on July 21, 2024, twenty-four days after his disastrous debate, Joe Biden was forced by his own party to suspend his campaign for a second term.

President Biden and Vice President Kamala Harris in March 2021. After Biden dropped out of the 2024 race, the Democrats chose Harris to be their presidential candidate. On November 5, 2024, she lost to former President Donald Trump, who became only the second president to be elected to two nonconsecutive terms. The first was Grover Cleveland. (See chapter three.)

EPILOGUE

AS HEAD OF THE COUNTRY'S EXECUTIVE BRANCH, THE PRESIDENT influences every aspect of American life. As commander in chief of the armed forces, the president also has responsibility to protect the nation from foreign enemies.

The country is at risk if its chief executive is sick for weeks the way injured James Garfield was in 1881. It cannot afford to have a president whose decision-making ability is affected the way Woodrow Wilson's was in 1919.

Many presidents have been open about medical problems that interfered with their duties. But other presidents—or the people around them—have misled, covered up, or lied about their health.

WHY THEY LIED

Presidents have chosen to hide a medical problem because they thought it was in the country's best interest. Chester Arthur kept quiet about his Bright's disease out of concern that the news would upset a public getting over the shock of Garfield's assassination. Grover Cleveland feared his cancer diagnosis would trigger a financial crisis.

Some ailing presidents sought to prove that they were still fit to lead. During World War II, Franklin Roosevelt hid his physical issues so that he didn't lose the confidence of the nation's allies or embolden its enemies. Ronald Reagan and his aides showed him quickly returning to his normal duties even though his body hadn't recovered from his gunshot wound. They believed they needed to reassure the public and discourage foreign adversaries from taking advantage after the assassination attempt.

Presidents have had less noble reasons for secrecy, too. They wanted to win elections, and signs of illness or disability could hurt their chances. Many voters never realized that Roosevelt's health was as bad as it was, and he was reelected to a fourth term. John Kennedy hid his physical problems while promoting a vigorous and energetic image. He went on to victory. Countering concerns about his age, Reagan aimed to appear hearty and robust. He was elected twice. But publicized reports about a medical condition derailed the reelection plans of Woodrow Wilson and Joe Biden.

Presidents have kept serious illnesses secret to maintain power and prevent the vice president from taking over. This has been especially true when the vice president was chosen to gain support from a rival faction of the party. Tensions and disagreements between the two camps tended to continue, as they did during the administrations of Presidents Garfield, Cleveland, and Kennedy.

White House spouses and aides sometimes helped with the deceptions. When Cleveland was recovering from cancer surgery, his wife told people that he was on vacation. Reagan's wife engineered photo sessions when he was ailing so that he looked better than he was. She also convinced the press secretary to downplay her husband's medical issues. Biden's staff restricted his schedule to hide his declining physical and mental condition. His wife frequently led him away from reporters and directed his movements during public appearances. Wilson's wife and closest aides went even further by concealing his state of health so that they could continue to make decisions in his name.

Many cover-ups would not have been possible without assistance from the president's physician. Doctors consider it unethical to share personal medical information unless the patient gives permission. But a few presidential physicians told outright lies.

The surgeons who operated on Grover Cleveland assured reporters that he had undergone simple dental work and suffered from a touch of rheumatism. More than two decades later, after Cleveland's death, one of the surgeons finally disclosed the truth to set the historical record straight.

When asked by the cabinet, Woodrow Wilson's physician refused to say that the president was too disabled to perform his duties. Meanwhile, Wilson was incapacitated by a stroke.

Some presidential physicians have deceived the public to protect their own reputations. James Garfield's principal doctor botched his care and was defensive when anyone criticized him. His misleading comments about Garfield's condition made the physician appear more competent than he was.

Like Garfield's doctor, Warren Harding's physician did not practice up-to-date medical techniques. Handpicked by Harding's wife, the man misdiagnosed and poorly treated the president. To shield himself from criticism, he kept other doctors away from Harding and lied to the press about the president's illness.

Franklin Roosevelt's presidential physician neglected to call in a cardiologist until the family insisted. He continued to give positive medical reports to the public even as Roosevelt's health declined.

One of John Kennedy's doctors helped him to hide his Addison's disease, intentionally misinforming the press and the public. She clashed with Kennedy's other physicians who objected to her drug treatments.

KEEPING THE SECRET

The press has a front row seat to the president's activities and behavior. Its job is to tell Americans about things they can't witness themselves.

At times, reporters have been skeptical of White House statements about a president's health. They asked more questions and dug deeper to discover the truth. During Chester Arthur's administration, for example, they tried to find out about his apparent illnesses but couldn't break through the barrier of silence around him.

Yet often the media have been too willing to believe a lie. Rather than investigating a White House deception, they guarded the secret.

When a reporter unearthed and published the details about Grover Cleveland's surgery, he was discredited and silenced by many in the press at the bidding of Cleveland's friends.

Journalists who reported on Franklin Roosevelt agreed not to shoot photographs or write stories about his paralysis. Although they observed Roosevelt's deteriorating condition, they didn't inform the public.

Reporters failed to reveal what they'd privately seen of Joe Biden's cognitive and physical decline. When one newspaper published an exposé, some members of the press joined the Biden administration in attacking it. Many news outlets never reported on the president's state of health until millions of viewers saw the evidence for themselves during the disastrous debate.

As technology evolves, the role of White House correspondents as eyewitnesses and investigators becomes even more important. AI-generated video and audio can be used as political propaganda to mislead the public about a president's health. Through accurate and impartial reporting, the press has the power to counteract such disinformation.

IF ONLY . . .

Of the eight presidents who died in office, a few suffered from conditions that would have been effectively prevented and treated today.

The first chief executive to die was William Henry Harrison, in 1841, after being president for only one month. Although early-nineteenth-century diagnoses aren't necessarily accurate, it is thought that Harrison died from pneumonia or possibly typhoid fever. Zachary Taylor, the second to die, in 1850, succumbed to a gastrointestinal illness, perhaps dysentery. Today's antibiotics would have cleared up those ailments. Better sanitation in Washington would have prevented typhoid fever and dysentery in the first place; both are intestinal diseases spread from human sewage.

An 1846 print illustrates the death of William Henry Harrison on April 4, 1841, one month after becoming president.

After James Garfield was shot in 1881, he was taken to the White House. Doctors believed he'd receive better care there than at a hospital. One hundred years later, the Secret Service

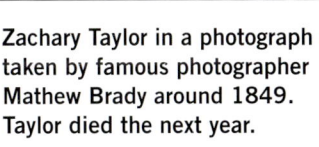

Zachary Taylor in a photograph taken by famous photographer Mathew Brady around 1849. Taylor died the next year.

The assassination of William McKinley on September 6, 1901, at the Pan-American Exposition in Buffalo, New York

rushed Ronald Reagan to a hospital trauma center equipped to deal with catastrophic injuries.

The assassin's bullet missed Garfield's vital organs and ended up harmlessly in fatty tissue. He died eighty days after his shooting from a massive infection caused by his physicians' unsterilized fingers and medical instruments. Reagan's 1981 wound was much more serious. His lung had been pierced by a bullet, and he would have died if he hadn't received immediate surgery. His doctors were better trained than Garfield's, and X-rays helped them locate the bullet. Antiseptics, sterile instruments and hands, and antibiotics minimized Reagan's infections, helping to save his life.

William McKinley was shot in the abdomen by an assassin in 1901. He developed an infection and died eight days after the shooting. Some historians believe antibiotics and a more skilled surgeon could have saved him. Others think McKinley wouldn't have lived even today, because of the bullet's damage to his pancreas and because he had a preexisting heart condition that complicated his recovery.

Warren Harding and Franklin Roosevelt died of cardiovascular disease. Their lives would have been extended by today's medications and devices that control high blood pressure and heart disease. Modern surgery can correct many cardiovascular issues. Both Harding and Roosevelt were heavy smokers, a habit that likely contributed to their health problems.

Abraham Lincoln and John Kennedy, both assassinated by a shot to the head, would be unlikely to survive their devastating injuries today despite modern improvements in trauma care.

QUESTIONS REMAIN

We might never learn how often a president's illness or medications affected his judgment, important decisions he made, or his interaction with foreign leaders. Yet no law requires presidential candidates or sitting presidents to take a physical or cognitive test to ensure that they are capable of performing their duties. No law forces them to release personal health reports. Recent presidents and candidates have provided some limited information because voters tell pollsters that they want to know. For decades, there have been calls for legal mandates.

In 1960, John Roosevelt proposed that presidential candidates must undergo a medical examination and share the results. (See chapter seven.) More than sixty years later, Nikki Haley called for a cognitive assessment to check the mental acuity of all candidates older than seventy-five. (See chapter nine.)

The history of White House medical secrets raises questions:

★ Is the president's right to privacy more important than the public's right to know medical details?

★ Should there be a level of physical and cognitive fitness required to serve as president?

★ Should there be an upper age limit for the presidency just as there is a minimum age of thirty-five?

★ Should certain conditions be disqualifying, such as incurable cancer even if it's controlled or in remission? What about depression and substance abuse?

★ Should a president be required to have an annual physical with the results disclosed?

★ Should that physical be conducted by an independent committee of doctors, not the president's regular physician?

★ If a president takes medications, should they be made public?

This book has told the stories of nine presidents who hid a medical crisis. Some commentators have suggested that other presidents secretly suffered from alcoholism and depression. In past centuries, such conditions were not recognized or diagnosed. More recent accounts are based on rumors or personal opinions. Because these cases are hard to confirm, they are not included here.

Several chief executives have experienced serious, even life-threatening illnesses but were more transparent about their health than the nine in this book. Those well-documented situations are explored in *The President Is Ailing: Tales of Sickness in the White House* (Calkins Creek, 2027).

Additional White House medical cover-ups may come to light in the future. A quarter century passed before the public heard the whole truth about Grover Cleveland's shipboard surgery. Details about John Kennedy's ailments have trickled out over many decades. Someday a lost document or forgotten diary may be found, revealing a new medical secret that changes our view of presidential history.

TIMELINE

1787
U.S. Constitution is written and signed. The states ratify it in 1788, and it goes into effect in 1789.

1792
Congress passes the first Presidential Succession Act.

1923
Warren Harding (1921–1923) dies. Vice President Calvin Coolidge succeeds him (1923–1929).

1919
Woodrow Wilson (1913–1921) has an incapacitating stroke.

1893
Grover Cleveland (1885–1889 and 1893–1897) has secret cancer surgery.

1917–1918
United States fights in the Great War (World War I).

1901
William McKinley (1897–1901) is assassinated. Vice President Theodore Roosevelt succeeds him (1901-1909).

1941–1945
United States fights in World War II.

1945
Franklin Roosevelt (1933–1945) dies. Vice President Harry Truman succeeds him (1945–1953).

1967
Twenty-Fifth Amendment is ratified.

1947
Congress passes the third Presidential Succession Act.

1963
John Kennedy (1961–1963) is assassinated. Vice President Lyndon Johnson succeeds him (1963–1969).

1974
Richard Nixon (1969–1974) resigns. Vice President Gerald Ford succeeds him (1974–1977).

1841

William Henry Harrison (1841) dies after one month in office. Vice President John Tyler succeeds him (1841–1845).

1850

Zachary Taylor (1849–1850) dies in office. Vice President Millard Fillmore succeeds him (1850–1853).

1886

Congress passes the second Presidential Succession Act.

1881

James Garfield (1881) is assassinated. Vice President Chester Arthur succeeds him (1881–1885).

1865

Abraham Lincoln (1861–1865) is assassinated. Vice President Andrew Johnson succeeds him (1865–1869).

1861–1865

American Civil War

1981

Ronald Reagan (1981–1989) survives an assassination attempt.

2024

Joseph Biden (2021–2025) drops his bid for reelection.

GLOSSARY

abdominal: referring to the abdomen, or the area of the body between the chest and pelvis.

abscess: a swelling caused by a collection of pus.

Addison's disease: a rare, chronic condition in which the **adrenal glands** do not produce enough hormones. Symptoms include fatigue, poor appetite, nausea, and muscle and joint pain. Can be life-threatening if not treated.

adrenal glands: glands above the kidneys that produce hormones to help regulate body functions such as blood pressure, heart function, immune system, and response to stress.

adrenaline: a hormone produced by the adrenal glands that prepares the body to react to stress or danger by increasing the heart rate.

Alzheimer's disease: a brain disorder that gradually destroys thinking skills, memory, and reasoning.

amphetamines: stimulant drugs.

anesthesia: use of drugs to stop a patient from feeling pain during surgery.

aneurysm: an abnormal bulge in the wall of a blood vessel that can lead to death if it ruptures.

antibiotic: a drug used to destroy disease-causing bacteria.

antiseptic: preventing the growth of microbes; a substance that kills harmful microbes.

appendicitis: inflammation of the **appendix**, a small organ in the lower right abdomen. Symptoms include pain, fever, and nausea.

arteriosclerosis: the thickening or hardening of artery walls which restricts blood circulation.

autoimmune disease: a condition in which the immune system attacks the body instead of protecting it.

autopsy (postmortem): the examination of a body to determine cause of death.

bacteria: microscopic one-celled organisms.

Bright's disease: a kidney disease known today as nephritis, or inflammation of the kidneys. Symptoms include blood in the urine, high blood pressure, fatigue, and swelling.

bronchitis: inflammation of the lungs' bronchial tubes causing a cough, chest pain, and shortness of breath.

cardiologist: a doctor who specializes in the heart and blood vessels.

cardiovascular system: having to do with the heart and circulation.

cauterize: to burn part of the body to stop bleeding or remove harmful tissue.

cerebral hemorrhage (once called **cerebral apoplexy**): stroke, sudden bleeding in the brain from a burst blood vessel.

cognitive: having to do with mental activity, such as thinking and remembering.

colitis: inflammation of the colon that causes diarrhea, bleeding, and pain.

colon: large intestine.

colonoscopy: a medical procedure that allows a doctor to view the inside of the colon by using a long flexible tube with a camera at the end.

cortisone: a drug used to reduce inflammation.

digitalis: a drug used to treat heart problems.

dysentery: an intestinal disease. Symptoms include abdominal pain, vomiting, and severe, often bloody diarrhea.

ether: a chemical used to put a patient to sleep during surgery.

gallbladder: a small sac under the liver that stores bile until it is needed for fat digestion.

gastrointestinal: having to do with the digestive system, including stomach and intestines.

gout: a condition that causes painful, inflamed joints.

hepatitis: inflammation of the liver. Symptoms include fever, pain, jaundice.

hormone: a chemical substance that regulates body functions.

hypertension: high blood pressure; can lead to stroke, heart attack, and other health problems.

inflammation: the body's response to infection or injury that may include swelling, redness, pain.

influenza (flu): a viral respiratory disease. Symptoms include fever, muscle aches, sore throat, runny nose, sneezing, and cough.

jaundice: yellowing of the skin and whites of the eyes.

malaria: an infectious disease caused by parasitic microbes transmitted by mosquitoes. Symptoms include fever and chills.

measles: an extremely contagious viral disease. Symptoms include fever and red spots on the skin.

microbe: microscopic organism, such as a bacterium or virus.

morphine: an addictive drug derived from opium that induces sleep and dulls pain.

nausea: a sick feeling in the stomach with the urge to vomit.

neurological: medical field dealing with the nervous system.

nitrous oxide (laughing gas): a gas used as a sedative and pain reducer in dentistry and other fields of medicine.

pancreas: organ that aids in digestion.

pathologist: a person who is medically trained to detect and diagnose disease by examining the body and its tissues and fluids.

pelvis: the lower part of the human body's trunk below the waist at the top of the legs; the hip area.

pneumonia: a lung infection with symptoms of cough, chest pain, rapid breathing, fever.

poliomyelitis (polio): a highly infectious viral disease that can cause permanent paralysis; preventable by a vaccine first introduced in the 1950s.

polyps: small growths which can occur on the lining of the intestine or elsewhere in the body.

prostate gland: part of the male reproductive system located in the pelvis below the bladder.

prosthesis: an artificial body part.

ptomaine (food) poisoning: an illness caused by ingesting food or drink contaminated by bacteria. Symptoms include stomach pain, vomiting, and diarrhea.

pus: thick fluid formed during an infection, consisting of bacteria mixed with dead white blood cells and tissue.

rheumatism: joint pain and stiffness.

scarlet fever: a bacterial disease usually seen in children. Symptoms include a red rash on the skin, sore throat, and fever.

shock: a medical condition that occurs when blood flow throughout the body is reduced. Symptoms include rapid heartbeat, shallow breathing, and sweating.

stroke: damage to the brain when its blood flow is interrupted due to a blocked or burst blood vessel.

tuberculosis: a serious and sometimes fatal lung disease caused by a bacterium. Symptoms include coughing, fever, fatigue, and chest pain.

typhoid fever: a disease caused by bacteria that spread through food and water contaminated with body waste. Symptoms include fever, headache, and intestinal bleeding.

urination: removal of liquid body waste from the bladder.

vaccine: a special preparation of killed or weakened microbes that triggers the body to produce immunity to a disease.

vertebrae: the bones that make up the spinal column.

MORE TO EXPLORE

In addition to the sources listed in the bibliography, check out the following for information.

Websites active at time of publication

THE PRESIDENTS

American Experience: The Presidents
pbs.org/wgbh/americanexperience/collections/presidents
The collection includes resources about several presidents, including those featured in this book. Watch documentaries and film clips. Find film transcripts and read interesting articles about each president's career.

The American Presidency Project, UC Santa Barbara
presidency.ucsb.edu
Search the archives for presidential speeches, press conferences, debates, documents, and biographical facts. The site includes links to historical video.

Gail Jarrow. *Ambushed!: The Assassination Plot Against President Garfield.* New York: Calkins Creek, 2021.
Read a young adult biography about James Garfield, including his rise to the presidency, his assassination, and his slow decline and death during the summer of 1881.

The White House Historical Association
whitehousehistory.org
Discover biographies of the presidents and first ladies. See images, listen to audio and podcasts, and watch videos about the White House and the people who lived there.

PRESIDENTIAL LIBRARIES AND MUSEUMS

with online resources and locations to visit

Grover Cleveland Birthplace Memorial Association, Caldwell, NJ
presidentcleveland.org

James A. Garfield National Historic Site, Mentor, OH
nps.gov/jaga

Warren G. Harding Presidential Sites, Marion, OH
hardingpresidentialsites.org

John F. Kennedy Presidential Library and Museum, Boston, MA
jfklibrary.org

Ronald Reagan Presidential Library and Museum, Simi Valley, CA
reaganlibrary.gov

Franklin D. Roosevelt Presidential Library and Museum, Hyde Park, NY
fdrlibrary.org

Woodrow Wilson Presidential Library and Museum, Staunton, VA
woodrowwilson.org
Woodrow Wilson House, Washington, DC
woodrowwilsonhouse.org

TWENTY-FIFTH AMENDMENT

American Experience: The American Vice President
pbs.org/wgbh/americanexperience/films/american-vice-president
This documentary explores the development and uses of the Twenty-Fifth Amendment, focusing on the unprecedented historical moments between 1963 and 1976. At the website, find articles about the American vice presidency and presidential succession.

Constitution Annotated
constitution.congress.gov
Read the Constitution in plain English with an explanation of each section.

Cynthia Levinson and Sanford Levinson. *Fault Lines in the Constitution: The Framers, Their Fights, and the Flaws That Affect Us Today.* Atlanta, GA: Peachtree Publishers, 2019.
In this young adult book, learn more about the Twenty-Fifth Amendment and the problems with presidential succession that the amendment didn't fix.

National Constitution Center
constitutioncenter.org/the-constitution/amendments/amendment-xxv
See more about the Presidential Disability and Succession Amendment at this site, including podcasts and essays by legal experts.

AUTHOR'S NOTE

AS A CHILD, I HAD A TWO-HUNDRED-AND-FIFTY-PIECE JIGSAW puzzle of the White House surrounded by portraits of each president. I used to spread out the pieces on the dining room table before methodically putting together the puzzle. I got faster every time I did it.

Thanks to that puzzle, I could name even the obscure presidents from the 1800s. I never heard about most of them in school. The only kids' books on presidents I'd seen were short biographies of the big names—Washington, Jefferson, Lincoln. The puzzle's last president was John Kennedy, who was in the White House then.

On Friday afternoon, November 22, 1963, a classmate on an errand to the principal's office brought back news he'd heard on the radio there. President Kennedy had been shot dead. The assassination and the assassin's televised killing became a topic of playground conversation for days.

I suddenly awoke to a world beyond my school and town. I began reading the daily newspaper and looking for books about Kennedy and other presidents. The seeds of my interest in history had been planted.

I enjoyed immersing myself in presidential history as I researched *White House Secrets*. Like the other three books in my Medical Fiascoes series (*Blood and Germs*, *Ambushed!*, *American Murderer*), it explores how disease impacted American history. This time I focused on hidden illnesses and the resulting fiascoes.

Throughout the past four decades, several historians have investigated the presidents' health. After studying their work, I identified chief executives who deliberately kept their medical conditions secret. I expected to feature nineteenth- and twentieth-century presidents. Then current events became history. After the June 2024 debate, I added the Biden chapter when damaging reports on his health surfaced and he withdrew from his reelection race.

To gather background on the nine presidents, I read biographies and watched documentaries that chronicled their lives and administrations. Books and articles by historians and political scientists provided more information. I found a range of opinions about each president's character, competency, and accomplishments, but I was most interested in the medical angle.

The bibliographies and citations in these secondary sources led me to primary sources where I verified facts and quotations. All scenes and dialogue described in my book are based on personal and eyewitness accounts in these primary sources. I discovered each president's own words in autobiographies, diaries, speeches, media interviews, and broadcasts. More details came from the memoirs, letters, and diaries of family and close colleagues. Although first-person viewpoints have obvious biases, these people had knowledge that outsiders did not.

A few physicians wrote about treating a president, usually after their famous patient's death. I read those reports in memoirs, old issues of medical journals, government documents, and court testimony.

The presidential libraries and museums, the Library of Congress, and the National Archives offered a wealth of material, including digitized documents and photographs.

Adding my own experiences to this research made it easier to write about these leaders. For example, visiting presidents' former homes gave me insight into their lives. I have memories of three of the nine highlighted presidents during the years they were in the White House.

I saw Ronald Reagan up close when he campaigned in my New Hampshire town. In 1981, I followed breaking news of the assassination attempt against him. To reassure the public, Reagan's aides minimized the seriousness of his condition. Their efforts worked on me. I never realized how close to death Reagan had been until I researched the chapter about him.

Along with more than 50 million other people, I watched the unedited June 2024 broadcast of the Biden–Trump debate. I didn't have to rely on historians or secondhand media reporting to summarize or interpret the event for me.

The medical crises in this book were tragic and sometimes avoidable. We all know that feeling sick affects everything you do. It's hard to concentrate on assignments, a test, or your teacher's lecture. You have trouble recalling what you've read or heard. Making decisions is a struggle. Presidents are no different. But their actions can affect hundreds of millions of people.

That's why the public deserves the truth about a chief executive's health. If the White House isn't willing to provide the information, the media have the duty to investigate and report honestly. The medical condition of the president mattered in 1881. It's even more important today.

—GJ

ACKNOWLEDGMENTS

I'M GRATEFUL TO THE FOLLOWING PEOPLE WHO HELPED ME find resources, understand information, and confirm facts: Cynthia Levinson; Sanford Levinson; Apurva Gunturu; Tate Jarrow; archivists at the John F. Kennedy Presidential Library and Museum and the Franklin D. Roosevelt Presidential Library and Museum; and the staffs at the James A. Garfield National Historic Site, the Warren G. Harding Presidential Sites, the Woodrow Wilson Presidential Library and Museum, and the Cornell University Library.

I appreciate the team at Calkins Creek/Astra Books for Young Readers for carefully and creatively turning my manuscript into a book and sending it out into the world. Special thanks go to Carolyn P. Yoder, my longtime editor, who shepherded *White House Secrets* from my proposal to published book. Her expertise and high standards keep me on my toes and make me a better writer.

—GJ

SOURCE NOTES

The source of each quotation in this book is found below. The citation indicates the first words of the quotation and its document source. The sources are listed either in the bibliography or here.

Websites active at time of publication

The following abbreviations are used:

TRIAL: *Report of the Proceedings in the Case of the United States vs. Charles J. Guiteau*
WILSON PAPERS: *The Papers of Woodrow Wilson Digital Edition*, Charlottesville: University of Virginia Press, Rotunda, 2017

CHAPTER ONE
DOOMED BY DIRTY FINGERS—JAMES GARFIELD (PAGE 12)

"What have I . . .": quoted in C. A. Edson, p. 613.
"wrecked the once . . .": letter, Guiteau to the American people, June 16, 1881, in TRIAL, p. 216.
"My God! What . . .": quoted by James Blaine, same as above, p. 121.
"I did it, and . . .": quoted by Patrick Kearney, same as above, p. 187.
"If I can't save . . .": quoted in "Doctors Disagreeing," *Chicago Tribune*, July 4, 1881.
"The President has passed . . .": "Official Bulletins of the President's Case," July 16, 1881, 7:00 p.m., p. 302.
"doing excellently.": same as above, July 21, 1881, 8:30 a.m., p. 302.
"looking very well" and "discharged several ounces . . .": same as above, "To the Consulting Surgeons—7 P.M.," July 22, 1881, p. 303.
"a general feeling . . .": "On the Brink," *St. Paul* [MN] *Daily Globe*, August 17, 1881.
"The people of the . . .": quoted in "Exchange Scintillations," *South Kentuckian*, August 30, 1881.
"has made some . . .": "Official Bulletins of the President's Case," September 15, 1881, 9:00 a.m., p. 326.
"Oh my! Swaim, what . . .": quoted in Reyburn, p. 95.
"Mrs. Garfield," and "the President . . .": Bliss, p. 304.
"I deny . . .": TRIAL, p. 226.
"His death . . .": same as above, p. 264.

CHAPTER TWO
THE HIDDEN DIAGNOSIS—CHESTER ARTHUR (PAGE 34)

"I have not been . . .": quoted in "The President in Washington," *New-York Tribune*, April 23, 1883.

"I expect President Arthur . . .": letter Guiteau to the American people, June 16, 1881, in TRIAL, p. 216.

"It was a common . . .": Andrew Dickson White, *Autobiography of Andrew Dickson White*, Vol. 1. New York: Century Co., 1905, p. 193.

"The death of . . .": diary entry, July 3, 1881, in Rutherford Birchard Hayes, *Diary and Letters of Rutherford Birchard Hayes, Nineteenth President of the United States*, Vol. 4, edited by Charles Richard Williams. Columbus: Ohio State Archaeological and Historical Society, 1925, p. 23.

"No man ever . . .": "President Arthur," *New York Times*, September 21, 1881.

"Any stories of the . . .": quoted in "President Arthur," *Helena* [MT] *Weekly Herald*, October 12, 1882.

"has been far from . . .": "The President Not Well," *New York Times*, March 11, 1883.

"How are you feeling?": quoted in "The President in Washington," *New-York Tribune*, April 23, 1883.

"I haven't been sick . . .": same as above.

"a long ride . . .": same as above.

"Their sensational . . .": same as above.

"a slight attack . . .": same as above.

"a slight attack . . .": same as above.

"His great physical . . .": Dr. George Peters, in "Ex-President Arthur Dead," *Evening Star* [DC], November 18, 1886.

"He was one of the few . . .": "Chester A. Arthur," *New York Times*, November 19, 1886.

"No man ever . . ." and "and no one ever . . .": Alexander McClure, *Recollections of Half a Century*, Salem, MA: Salem Press Company, 1902, p. 115.

CHAPTER THREE
THE VANISHING PRESIDENT—GROVER CLEVELAND (PAGE 54)

"Whatever you . . .": telegram from Cleveland to Charles W. Goodyear, July 23, 1884, in Nevins, *Letters of Grover Cleveland*, p. 37.

"Were it . . ." and "I would have . . .": Keen, p. 31.

"If you hit . . .": quoted in Nevins, *Grover Cleveland: A Study in Courage*, based on a 1931 interview with Dr. John Erdmann, p. 530.

"What a sigh . . .": Keen, p. 40.

"Had He a Cancer?": "Had He a Cancer?," *Grand Rapids* [MI] *Herald*, July 8, 1893.

"Cleveland Ill.": "Cleveland Ill," *Public Daily Ledger* [Maysville, KY], July 7, 1893.

"the report is accepted . . .": "Had He a Cancer?," *Grand Rapids* [MI] *Herald*, July 8, 1893.

"The President is all right . . .": "Not Seriously Ill," *Evening Star* [DC], July 7, 1893.

"The president is laid up . . .": quoted in "President Cleveland Better," *Washington Post*, July 8, 1893.

"has much improved . . .": same as above.

"My God, Olney . . .": quoted in Nevins, *Grover Cleveland: A Study in Courage*, p. 532.

"Cleveland was doing . . ." and "His illness . . .": "Cleveland Improving," *News* [Providence, RI], July 10, 1893.

"Whatever you do, tell . . .": telegram from Cleveland to Charles W. Goodyear, July 23, 1884, in Nevins, *Letters of Grover Cleveland*, p. 37.

"He came here . . ." and "and with an unusually . . .": letter from Frances F. Cleveland to Governor William E. Russell, July 31, 1893, in Nevins, *Letters of Grover Cleveland*, p. 329.

"It is useless . . .": "The President a Very Sick Man," *Philadelphia Press*, August 29, 1893, reprinted in "The President's Health," *New-York Daily Tribune*, August 30, 1893.

"it regarded . . .": "President Cleveland's Condition," *Indianapolis Journal*, September 1, 1893.

"weak" and "frothy" and "vain" and "It is a serious . . .": "A Very Alarming Rumor," *Seattle Post-Intelligencer*, August 30, 1893.

"I saw nothing . . .": quoted in "Interview with Dr Hasbrouck," *New-York Tribune*, August 30, 1893.

"a crime . . .": "A Crime Against Decency," *Washington Post*, September 13, 1893, quoting from the *St. Louis Globe-Democrat*.

"a most astounding . . .": letter from Cleveland to Thomas F. Bayard, September 11, 1893, in Nevins, *Letters of Grover Cleveland*, p. 334.

"I have tried . . .": quoted in Nevins, *Grover Cleveland: A Study in Courage*, p. 763.

"It was of the utmost . . ." and "Few Americans . . .": quoted in "How Vital
State Secret Was Kept," *Sunday Star* [DC], September 30, 1917.

CHAPTER FOUR
MISSING IN ACTION—WOODROW WILSON (PAGE 78)

"I seem to have . . .": quoted in "From the Diary of Dr. Grayson,"
September 26, 1919, WILSON PAPERS, Vol. 63, p. 519.

"Please get Doctor . . .": quoted in Hoover, p. 101.

"He looked as if . . ." and "There was not a sign . . .": Hoover, p. 102.

"The world must . . .": "An Address to a Joint Session of Congress,"
April 2, 1917, in WILSON PAPERS, Vol. 41, p. 525.

"he was never the same . . .": Hoover, p. 99.

"The League . . ." and "and if it fails . . .": quoted in Grayson, p. 95.

"was on the verge . . .": Grayson, p. 99.

"I have never been . . ." and "and I just feel . . .": quoted in "From the Diary
of Dr. Grayson," September 26, 1919, WILSON PAPERS, Vol. 63, p. 519.

"The President is . . ." and "absolute rest . . .": quoted in "Text of the Official
White House Bulletin; Absolute Rest Remedy," *Washington Post*,
October 3, 1919.

"worry and strain.": "'Very Sick Man,' Says Grayson of President in Late
Night Bulletin," *Washington Post*, October 3, 1919.

"I have read . . .": Tumulty, p. 443.

"While Woodrow Wilson . . .": Tumulty, p. 444.

"was his mind clear or not": quoted in "A Memorandum by Dr. Grayson,
October 6, 1919," WILSON PAPERS, Vol. 64, p. 496.

"was very much annoyed . . .": "A Memorandum by Dr. Grayson,
October 6, 1919," WILSON PAPERS, Vol. 64, p. 496.

"all this secrecy . . .": Senator Spencer quoted in "A Memorandum by Robert
Lansing, December 4, 1919," in WILSON PAPERS, Vol. 64, p. 123.

"like a stone wall . . .": Grayson, 53.

"Every time you . . ." and "you are turning . . .": quoted in Wilson, *My
Memoir*, p. 289.

"How can I protect . . .": same as above.

"Have everything come . . .": same as above.

"Wilson's Last Mad Act" and "When the country . . .": "Wilson's Last Mad
Act," *Los Angeles Times*, February 15, 1920.

"This combination . . ." and "The president thinks . . .": "The American
Regency," *Chicago Daily Tribune*, February 28, 1920.

"I have been thinking . . .": Grayson, p. 114.

"a shadow of his . . .": Hoover, p. 103.

"The machinery . . .": Grayson, p. 139.

"Up to the time . . ." and "might lead . . .": "Wilson Had Stroke in 1919 Collapse," *New York Times*, February 4, 1924.

CHAPTER FIVE
THE DEADLY VOYAGE—WARREN HARDING (PAGE 100)

"I am tired.": from *Joel T. Boone Papers—Memoirs*, Library of Congress, Washington, DC, Chapter 20, p. 7, quoted in Heller, p. 60.

"I am not fit . . .": quoted in Nicholas Murray Butler, *Across the Busy Years: Recollections and Reflections*, Vol. 1. New York: Charles Scribner's Sons, 1939, p. 411.

"normalcy": Harding, "Back to Normal" address, May 14, 1920.

"I think that . . .": letter from Warren Harding to Dr. Charles Sawyer, March 15, 1916, Charles E. Sawyer Papers, quoted in Ferrell, *The Strange Deaths of President Harding*, p. 1.

"I don't believe there is . . . ": quoted in "Harding Declares Return to Normalcy Big Result of Year," *New York Times*, March 5, 1922.

"How are things . . .": from *Joel T. Boone Papers—Memoirs*, Library of Congress, Washington, DC, chapter 19, p. 106, quoted in Heller, p. 58.

"Not at all well . . .": same as above.

"Of course, we . . .": from *Joel T. Boone Papers—Memoirs*, Library of Congress, Washington, DC , chapter 20, p. 3, quoted in Heller, p. 59.

"promptly be restored . . .": Dr. Work quoted in "Harding Has Attack of Ptomaine Poison: Drops Yosemite Trip," *New York Times*, July 29, 1923.

"I will not be . . .": from *Joel T. Boone Papers—Memoirs*, Library of Congress, Washington, DC, chapter 20, p. 26, quoted in Heller, p. 62.

"temporarily overstrained . . .": "President Harding's Last Illness, Official Bulletins of Attending Physicians," *Journal of the American Medical Association*, Vol. 81 (August 18, 1923), p. 603.

"His condition is grave.": same as above.

"that Presidents owe . . .": "Hughes Can Call Cabinet," *New York Times*, July 31, 1923.

"Inability to discharge . . .": U.S. Constitution, Article II, Section 1, Clause 6.

"the duty of the . . .": "Hughes Can Call Cabinet," *New York Times*, July 31, 1923.

"I think I may . . .": quoted in "Faces a Slow Recovery," *New York Times*, August 2, 1923.

"was not doing . . .": from *Joel T. Boone Papers—Memoirs*, Library of Congress, Washington, DC, chapter 20, pp. 44–46, quoted in Heller, p. 65.

"It looks as though . . .": quoted in Wilbur, p. 381.

"there is every indication . . .": quoted in "Faces a Slow Recovery," *New York Times*, August 2, 1923.

"We are more confident . . .": "President Harding's Last Illness, Official Bulletins of Attending Physicians," *Journal of the American Medical Association*, Vol. 81 (August 18, 1923), p. 603.

"The President has had . . .": same as above.

"Now I feel . . .": from *Joel T. Boone Papers—Memoirs*, Library of Congress, Washington, DC, chapter 20, p. 52, quoted in Heller, p. 66.

"That's good. Go on.": "Harding's Death Stuns Nation; President Coolidge Sworn In," *Los Angeles Times*, August 3, 1923.

"It took nearly . . .": Wilbur, p. 382.

"died instantaneously . . .": "President Harding's Last Illness, Official Bulletins of Attending Physicians," *Journal of the American Medical Association*, Vol. 81 (August 18, 1923), p. 603.

"at any time.": same as above.

"The official reports . . .": Calvin Coolidge, *The Autobiography of Calvin Coolidge*, New York: Cosmopolitan Book Corporation, 1929, p. 173.

"Harding came to . . .": Wilbur, p. 378.

CHAPTER SIX
AN IMAGE MANIPULATED—FRANKLIN ROOSEVELT
(PAGE 124)

"Repetition does not . . .": Franklin D. Roosevelt, Radio Address to the New York Herald Tribune Forum, October 26, 1939.

"The United States of America . . ." and "Repetition does not . . .": same as above.

"You can say definitely . . .": Dr. George Draper, quoted in "F. D. Roosevelt Ill of Poliomyelitis," *New York Times*, September 16, 1921.

"If you had spent . . .": quoted in Schlesinger, *The Age of Roosevelt*, p. 406.

"than if he had . . .": James Farley, quoted in "Says Roosevelt Is Made Target of 'Whisperers,'" *New York Times*, July 31, 1932.

"temporary, partial . . .": Dr. Francis E. Fronczak, quoted in "'Roosevelt is Robust' Says Buffalo Doctor," *New York Times*, October 23, 1932.

"he is bearing . . .": "The President's Good Health," *New York Herald Tribune*, January 27, 1934.

"a date which will . . .": "Address of the President to the Congress of the United States," December 8, 1941, Franklin D. Roosevelt Presidential Library and Museum.

"was in better health . . ." and "above-average stamina.": "At 62," *Time*, February 7, 1944.

"For a man of 62 . . .": quoted in "President's Condition Called Good," *Washington Post*, April 5, 1944.

"excellent in all respects" and "better than the average . . .": quoted in Charles Hurd, "President's Health 'Excellent,' Admiral McIntire Reports," *New York Times*, June 9, 1944.

"It was widely . . .": James A. Farley to the editor of *New York Times*, March 1, 1951, "New Amendment Discussed," *New York Times*, March 5, 1951.

"the people who . . ." and "a whispering campaign": Robert E. Hannegan quoted in "Whispering Drive Seen by Hannegan," *New York Times*, October 14, 1944.

"he was in pretty . . .": "Health Pretty Good, Roosevelt Declares," *New York Times*, October 18, 1944.

"one of the principal . . ." and "is not in fit . . .": "Mr. Roosevelt's Health," *Chicago Daily Tribune*, October 17, 1944.

"was shocked by . . .": Truman, p. 2.

"I hope that you will . . .": White House transcript of "Radio Broadcast of Report to Congress on Crimea Conference," March 1, 1945, Franklin D. Roosevelt Presidential Library and Museum.

"He looks in excellent . . .": "Radio Broadcast of Report to Congress on Crimea Conference," March 1, 1945, audio, Franklin D. Roosevelt Presidential Library and Museum.

"Plainly, he was . . .": Truman, p. 3.

"For more than 12 . . .": Jack Stinnett, "Stinnett Hears FDR Is Out in '48; Will Not Be Candidate," *Daily Alaska Empire*, March 27, 1945.

"You're going to like . . .": quoted in "Did U.S. Elect a Dying President? The Inside Facts of the Final Weeks of FDR," *U.S. News & World Report*, March 23, 1951, p. 20.

"I have a terrific . . .": Margaret Suckley, Oral History, Franklin D. Roosevelt Presidential Library, quoted in Goodwin, p. 602.

"appeared to be . . .": "Roosevelt Health Long Under Doubt," *New York Times*, April 13, 1945.

"excellent condition . . .": McIntire, p. 17.

"in splendid shape.": quoted in "Everybody Knew it But the People,"
    Saturday Evening Post, May 19, 1945, p. 108.
"the state of Mr. Roosevelt's . . ." and "it must not . . .": same as above.

CHAPTER SEVEN
TARNISHED HERO—JOHN KENNEDY (PAGE 148)

"I'm the healthiest . . .": quoted in O'Donnell, p. 7.
"Kennedy, Tan . . .": "Kennedy, Tan and Fit, Returns to His Office,"
    Washington Post and Times Herald, May 24, 1955.
"At least one half . . .": Robert Kennedy, in Meyers, p. vi.
"No one who has . . .": Schlesinger, *A Thousand Days*, p. 19.
"a depletion of adrenal . . .": letter from Janet Travell to John Kennedy,
    July 21, 1959, Papers of John F. Kennedy Library, Pre-Presidential
    Papers, Presidential Campaign Files.
"adrenal insufficiency": same as above.
"above-average . . .": same as above.
"back is entirely well": same as above.
"adrenal insufficiency": letter Cohen and Travell to Kennedy,
    June 11, 1960, Papers of John F. Kennedy Library, Pre-Presidential
    Papers, Presidential Campaign Files.
"that the Kennedy . . .": Pierre Salinger quoted by John Harris, in "Bob
    Says Brother's Health Is Excellent," *Boston Globe*, July 5, 1960.
"Youth and Vigor": *Kennedy for President* campaign pamphlet, 1960.
"depend on the health . . .": quoted in "FDR Son Asks Nominee Tell Health
    Record," *Daily News* [NY], November 4, 1960.
"I have never had . . ." and "no problem": "Transcript of President-elect's
    New Conference," *New York Times*, November 11, 1960.
"not much of a pill . . ." and "free of health . . .": Ernest Barcella, "New Man
    in the White House," *Today's Health*, Vol. 39 (February 1961), p. 78.
"more pills, potions . . .": Sorenson, p. 41.
"symbol of . . .": Sorenson, p. 368.
"No President . . ." and "has any business . . .": quoted in Boyce Rensberger,
    "Amphetamines Used By a Physician To Lift Moods of Famous Patients,"
    New York Times, December 4, 1972.

CHAPTER EIGHT
CHEATING DEATH—RONALD REAGAN (PAGE 178)

"If I'd had . . .": quoted in Nancy Reagan, *My Turn*, p. 12.

"I feel like . . .": quoted in Pekkanen.

"I'm not so sure . . .": Reagan, *An American Life*, p. 134.

"the public had a right . . .": quoted in Lawrence K. Altman, "Reagan Vows to Resign if Doctor In White House Finds Him Unfit," *New York Times*, June 11, 1980.

"If I were President . . .": same as above.

"What the hell's that?": Reagan, *An American Life*, p. 259.

"the smile just . . .": Michael Putzel, quoted in Lou Cannon, "The Shooting," *Washington Post*, March 31, 1981.

"Get off, I think . . .": Reagan, *An American Life*, p. 259.

"I feel so bad": quoted in Pekkanen.

"Honey, I forgot . . .": Nancy Reagan, p. 6.

"I hope you're . . .": Reagan, *An American Life*, p. 261.

"Today, Mr. President, we're . . .": same as above.

"he was never . . .": and "Probaby several inches.": quoted in "Excerpts From Transcript of Briefing on Wounds of President and Two Others," *New York Times*, March 31, 1981.

"as upbeat . . .": Lawrence K. Altman, "Physician Says Reports on Reagan Were Optimistic but Hid Nothing," *New York Times*, April 6, 1981.

"Mr. Reagan's life . . .": O'Leary quoted in Lawrence K. Altman, "Doctor Says President Lost More Blood Than Disclosed," *New York Times*, April 3, 1981.

"The loss of blood . . .": Joseph M. Giordano as told to Jack Nelson and Rudy Abramson, "Delay Could Have Been Fatal," *Los Angeles Times*, April 4, 1981.

"he was close . . .": Joseph Giordano, quoted in Rachel Muir, "Saving the President," *GW Today*, June 30, 2010.

"If I'd had . . .": quoted in Nancy Reagan, p. 12.

"Can we rewrite . . .": same as above, p. 11.

"There was no hurry . . .": Deaver, p. 141.

"a mild 'setback.'" quoted in Lawrence K. Altman, "Reagan's Condition Called 'Good'; He Sees Aides as Fever Goes Down," *New York Times*, April 5, 1981.

"The President was a lot . . .": quoted in Pekkanen.

"He was as close to death's door . . .": Maureen Reagan, p. 275.

"terrific": same as above, p. 276.

"his own strong . . .": Aaron, p. 1693.

"It would have . . .": and "giving them . . .": Speakes, p. 9.

"Whatever happens . . .": Reagan Diaries, Vol. 1, April 11, 1981, p. 31.

"I will not make . . .": October 21, 1984, Debate Transcript, The Commission on Presidential Debates. debates.org/voter-education/debate-transcripts/october-21-1984-debate-transcript/.

"I had cancer. I don't . . .": "President Ronald Reagan's remarks on questions by *Readers Digest* regarding to his cancer at Camp David, Maryland," July 27, 1985, at 2:23, National Archives, catalog.archives.gov/id/137880396.

"Sometimes you wonder . . .": Nancy Reagan, p. 282.

"honor of allowing me . . ." and "I now begin . . .": letter from Ronald Reagan to My Fellow Americans, November 5, 1994.

"to divulge accurate . . .": from Office of Ronald Reagan, in Oliver H. Beahrs, "The Medical History of President Ronald Reagan," *Journal of the American College of Surgeons*, Vol. 178 (January 1994), p. 86.

CHAPTER NINE
THE DISASTROUS DEBATE—JOE BIDEN (PAGE 204)

"No one's pushing . . .": quoted in Lauren Egan, Eli Stokols, Elena Schneider, and Jonathan Lemire, "Biden: 'No One's Pushing Me Out,'" *Politico*, July 3, 2024.

"Let's finish this job.": Joe Biden, "Joe Biden Launches His Campaign For President: Let's Finish the Job," YouTube video, youtube.com/watch?v=ChjibtX0UzU&t=13s.

"Make my day, pal.": Joe Biden (@JoeBiden), "Donald Trump lost two debates to me in 2020 . . .", May 15, 2024, X, x.com/JoeBiden/status/17907138878248038478.

"healthy, vigorous . . .": Kevin O'Connor, "Summary of Medical and Surgical History of Vice President Joseph R. Biden," December 15, 2019.

"nothing more than . . .": Kate Bedingfield, White House Communications Director, quoted in "Joe Biden Trips and Falls Three Times Boarding Air Force One," *Telegraph*, March 19, 2021.

"that President Biden . . .": WCVB-TV, "RFK Jr. a Holds News Conference After Biden Drops Out of 2024 Race," Associated Press, YouTube video, July 21, 2024, youtube.com/watch?v=LXrysxb8_m4&t=10s.

"He's in decline.": quoted in Ryan Hernández, "Dean Phillips and Nikki Haley Would Like to Remind You They Are (Relatively) Young," NOTUS, January 21, 2024, notus.org/2024-election/dean-phillips-nikki-haley-new-hampshire.

"No, I haven't taken . . .": quoted in Grace Segers, "Biden Says He Hasn't Taken a Cognitive Test: 'Why the Hell Would I Take a Test?'" *CBS News*, August 5, 2020.

"diminished faculties . . .": Special Counsel Robert K. Hur, *Report of the Special Counsel on the Investigation Into Unauthorized Removal, Retention, and Disclosure of Classified Document Discovered at Locations Including the Penn Biden Center and the Delaware Private Residence of President Joseph R. Biden, Jr.*, U.S. Department of Justice, Washington, DC, February 5, 2024, p. 242.

"a sympathetic, well-meaning . . .": same as above, p. 6.

"I'm well-meaning . . .": quoted in Matt Viser and Tyler Pager, "Biden Responds Angrily to Special Counsel Report Questioning His Memory," *Washington Post*, February 8, 2024.

"He continues to be . . .": Memorandum from Kevin O'Connor to Karine Jean-Pierre, February 28, 2024.

"He passes a cognitive test . . ." and "The president . . .": quoted in Haisten Willis, "White House: Biden 'Passes a Cognitive Test Every Day,'" *Washington Examiner*, February 28, 2024.

"Shame on all . . .": Dean Phillips (@deanphillips), "I'm attacked for being honest . . . ," February 6, 2024, X, x.com/deanbphillips/status/1754948258571407570.

"ran a sham primary.": "RFK Jr. Address to the Nation: Full Transcript," August 23, 2024, im1776.com/2024/08/24/rfk-address-to-the-nation/.

"cheap fakes videos": White House, "Press Briefing by Press Secretary Karine Jean-Pierre and National Security Communications Advisor John Kirby," June 17, 2024.

"Biden's Biggest . . .": *ABC News*, June 27, 2024, abcnews.go.com/538/bidens-biggest-weakness-age-full-display-thursday-debate-analysis/story?id=111500745.

"Inside Biden's Debate . . .": *Time*, June 28, 2024, time.com/6993760/joe-biden-debate-disaster-democratic-panic/.

"Biden's Disastrous . . .": *CNN*, June 28, 2024, cnn.com/2024/06/28/politics/biden-trump-presidential-debate-analysis/index.html.

"struggling to string . . .": Alex Thompson, "Two Joe Bidens: The Night America Saw the Other One," *Axios*, June 29, 2024.

"More than once . . .": Editorial Board, "To Serve His Country, President Biden Should Leave the Race," *New York Times*, June 28, 2024.

"When you get . . .": quoted in Andrew Restuccia, Siobhan Hughes, Ken Thomas, Catherine Lucey, and Tarini Parti, "Defiant Biden Hits Campaign Trail as Democrats Discuss Replacement," *Wall Street Journal*, June 28, 2024

"It [the debate] doesn't . . .": Elizabeth Sherwood-Randall, quoted in Peter Baker, David E. Sanger, Zolan Kanno-Youngs, and Katie Rogers, "Biden's Lapses Are Said to Be Increasingly Common and Worrisome," *New York Times*, July 2, 2024.

"He's inquisitive . . .": Neera Tanden, quoted in same as above.

"No one's pushing . . .": quoted in Lauren Egan, Eli Stokols, Elena Schneider, and Jonathan Lemire, "Biden: 'No One's Pushing Me Out,'" *Politico*, July 3, 2024.

"I'll do it" and "But no one . . .": White House, "Remarks by President Biden in Press Conference," July 11, 2024, whitehouse.gov/briefing-room/speeches-remarks/2024/07/11/remarks-by-president-biden-in-press-conference-9/.

"in the best interest . . .": letter from Joseph R. Biden, Jr., July 21, 2024, posted on @JoeBiden, x.com.

"the largest . . .": Speaker Mike Johnson (@SpeakerJohnson), "At this unprecedented juncture in American history . . . ," July 21, 2024, X, x.com/SpeakerJohnson/status/1815093011669516433.

"There's been no . . .": The White House, "Press Briefing by Press Secretary Karine Jean-Pierre," July 24, 2024, whitehouse.gov/briefing-room/press-briefings/2024/07/24/press-briefing-by-press-secretary-karine-jean-pierre-64/.

"A number of my . . ." and "I had a really, really . . .": interview with Robert Costa, "CBS Sunday Morning," *CBS News*, August 11, 2024.

"had shown signs . . .": Editorial Board, "Biden's Crowning Moment Came Before His Monday Speech," *Washington Post*, August 20, 2024.

"A coterie of powerful . . .": Maureen Dowd, "After Biden Bloodletting, Time for Fun!" *New York Times*, August 18, 2024.

BIBLIOGRAPHY

*Indicates primary sources

*Aaron, Benjamin L., MD, and S. David Rockoff, MD. "The Attempted Assassination of President Reagan: Medical Implications and Historical Perspective." *Journal of the American Medical Association*, Vol. 272 (December 7, 1994): 1689–93.

Abrams, Herbert L. *"The President Has Been Shot": Confusion, Disability, and the 25th Amendment in the Aftermath of the Attempted Assassination of Ronald Reagan*. New York: W. W. Norton, 1992.

Algeo, Matthew. *The President Is a Sick Man: Wherein the Supposedly Virtuous Grover Cleveland Survives a Secret Surgery at Sea and Vilifies the Courageous Newspaperman Who Dared Expose the Truth*. Chicago: Chicago Review Press, 2011.

Anthony, Carl Sferrazza. *Florence Harding: The First Lady, the Jazz Age, and the Death of America's Most Scandalous President*. New York: William Morrow and Company, 1998.

Asbell, Bernard. *When F. D. R. Died*. New York: Holt, Rinehart and Winston, 1961.

Barcella, Ernest. "New Man in the White House." *Today's Health*, Vol. 39 (February 1961): 22–27, 73–78.

Barrett, Laurence I. *Gambling With History: Ronald Reagan in the White House*. New York: Penguin Books, 1984.

*Beahrs, Oliver H. "The Medical History of President Ronald Reagan," *Journal of the American College of Surgeons*, Vol. 178 (January 1994): 86–96.

Berg, A. Scott. *Wilson*. New York: G. P. Putnam's Sons, 2013.

Beschloss, Michael R. *Presidential Courage: Brave Leaders and How They Changed America, 1789–1989*. New York: Simon & Schuster, 2007.

Blair, Joan, and Clay Blair. *The Search for JFK*. New York: Berkley Publishing, 1976.

*Bliss, D. W. "The Story of President Garfield's Illness, Told by the Physician in Charge." *Century Illustrated Monthly Magazine*, Vol. 23 (December 1881): 299–305.

*Brooks, John J., Horatio T. Enterline , and Gonzalo E. Aponte. "The Final Diagnosis of President Cleveland's Lesion." *Transactions & Studies of the College of Physicians of Philadelphi*a, Series 5, Vol. 2 (March 1980): 1–25.

*Bruenn, Howard G. "Clinical Notes on the Illness and Death of President Franklin D. Roosevelt." *Annals of Internal Medicine*, Vol. 72 (April 1970): 579–91.

Bumgarner, John R. *The Health of the Presidents: The 41 United States Presidents Through 1993 from a Physician's Point of View*. Jefferson, NC: McFarland & Company, 1994.

Burns, James MacGregor. *John Kennedy: A Political Profile*. New York: Harcourt, Brace, and World, 1960.

Crispell, Kenneth R., and Carlos F. Gomez. *Hidden Illness in the White House*. Durham, NC: Duke University Press, 1988.

Dallek, Robert. *An Unfinished Life: John F. Kennedy, 1917–1963*. Boston: Little, Brown, 2003.

Darman, Jonathan. *Becoming FDR: The Personal Crisis That Made a President*. New York: Random House, 2022.

*Deaver, Michael K. *A Different Drummer: My Thirty Years with Ronald Reagan*. New York: HarperCollins, 2001.

Dehler, Gregory J. *Chester Alan Arthur: The Life of a Gilded Age Politician and President*. New York: Nova Science Publishers, 2007.

Duckett, Kenneth W. "The Harding Papers: How Some Were Burned . . . " *American Heritage*, Vol. 16 (February 1965): 25–31, 102–109.

*Edson, C. A. "The Sickness and Nursing of President Garfield with Many Interesting Incidents Never Before Given to the Public." In *The Life of James Abram Garfield* by William Ralston Balch. Philadelphia: Hubbard Bros, 1881.

Engel, Jeffrey A., and Thomas J. Knock, eds. *When Life Strikes the President: Scandal, Death, and Illness in the White House.* New York: Oxford University Press, 2017.

*Esmarch, Friedrich. "Concerning the Treatment of the Wound of President Garfield." *Boston Medical and Surgical Journal*, Vol. 107 (September 7, 1882): 234–37.

Evans, Hugh E. *The Hidden Campaign: FDR's Health and the 1944 Election.* Armonk, NY: M. E. Sharpe, 2002.

Farquhar, Michael. *A Treasury of Deception: Liars, Misleaders, Hoodwinkers, and the Extraordinary True Stories of History's Greatest Hoaxes, Fakes, and Frauds.* New York: Penguin, 2005.

———. *A Treasury of Great American Scandals: Tantalizing True Tales of Historic Misbehavior by the Founding Fathers and Others Who Let Freedom Swing.* New York: Penguin Books, 2003.

Feerick, John D. *From Failing Hands: The Story of Presidential Succession.* New York: Fordham University Press, 1965.

———. *The Twenty-Fifth Amendment: Its Complete History and Applications*, 3rd ed. New York: Fordham University Press, 2014.

Ferrell, Robert H. *The Dying President: Franklin D. Roosevelt, 1944–45.* Columbia: University of Missouri Press, 1998.

———. *Ill-Advised: Presidential Health and Public Trust.* Columbia: University of Missouri Press, 1992.

———. *The Strange Deaths of President Harding.* Columbia: University of Missouri Press, 1996.

Gallagher, Hugh Gregory. *FDR's Splendid Deception.* New York: Dodd, Mead, 1985.

Garrison, Webb, and Beth Wieder. *A Treasury of White House Tales.* Nashville, TN: Rutledge Hill Press, 2002.

Gilbert, Robert E. *The Mortal Presidency: Illness and Anguish in the White House.* New York: Fordham University Press, 1998.

Goldberg, Edward Lewis. *Presidential Health Matters: The Medical History of the United States as Seen Through the Lives of Forty-Six Presidents*. San Diego, CA: Konstellation Press, 2023.

Goodwin, Doris Kearns. *No Ordinary Time: Franklin and Eleanor Roosevelt: The Home Front in World War II*. New York: Simon & Schuster, 1994.

Graff, Henry F. *Grover Cleveland*. New York: Times Books, 2002.

*Grayson, Rear Admiral Cary T. *Woodrow Wilson: An Intimate Memoir*. New York: Holt, Rinehart, and Winston, 1960.

Heckscher, August. *Woodrow Wilson*. New York: Charles Scribner's Sons, 1991.

*Heller, Milton F., Jr. *The Presidents' Doctor: An Insider's View of Three First Families*. New York: Vantage Press, 2000.

*Hoover, Irwin Hood. *Forty-Two Years in the White House*. Boston: Houghton Mifflin, 1934.

Howe, George Frederick. *Chester A. Arthur: A Quarter-Century of Machine Politics*. New York: Dodd, Mead & Company, 1934.

Jeffers, H Paul. *An Honest President: The Life and Presidencies of Grover Cleveland*. New York: William Morrow, 2000.

Kalt, Brian C. *Unable: The Law, Politics, and Limits of Section 4 of the Twenty-Fifth Amendment*. New York: Oxford University Press, 2019.

*Keen, William W. *The Surgical Operations on President Cleveland in 1893*. Philadelphia: George W. Jacobs & Company, 1917.

Kurland, Philip B., and Ralph Lerner, eds. *The Founders' Constitution*. Vol. 3, pp. 564–67. Chicago: University of Chicago Press, 1987.

Lachman, Charles. *A Secret Life: The Sex, Lies, and Scandals of President Grover Cleveland*. New York: Skyhorse Publishing, 2011.

*Lamb, D. S. "Report of the Post-Mortem Examination of the Body of Charles J. Guiteau." *Medical News*, Vol. 41 (July 8, 1882): 43–45.

Lomazow, Steven, and Eric Fettmann. *FDR's Deadly Secret*. New York: PublicAffairs, 2009.

MacMahon, Edward B., and Leonard Curry. *Medical Cover-Ups in the White House*. Washington, DC: Farragut Publishing, 1987.

Marmor, Michael F. "Wilson, Strokes, and Zebras." *New England Journal of Medicine*, Vol. 307 (August 26, 1982): 528–535.

Marrin, Albert. *FDR and the American Crisis*. New York: Alfred A. Knopf, 2014.

Martin, John Stuart. "When the President Disappeared." *American Heritage*, Vol. 8 (October 1957): 10–13, 102–103.

Marx, Rudolph. *The Health of the Presidents*. New York: G. P. Putnam's Sons, 1960.

*McClure, Alexander K. *Recollections of Half a Century*. Salem, MA: Salem Press Company, 1902.

McDermott, Rose. *Presidential Leadership, Illness, and Decision Making*. Cambridge, MA: Cambridge University Press, 2008.

McElroy, Robert McNutt. *Grover Cleveland: The Man and the Statesman, An Authorized Biography*. New York: Harper & Brothers, 1923.

*McIntire, Vice-Admiral Ross T. *White House Physician*. New York: G. P. Putnam's Sons, 1946.

Means, Gaston B. *The Strange Death of President Harding: From the Diaries of Gaston B. Means as Told to May Dixon Thacker*. New York: Guild Publishing Corporation, 1930.

*Meyers, Joan, ed. *John Fitzgerald Kennedy . . . As We Remember Him*. New York: Atheneum, 1965.

Moses, John B., and Wilbur Cross. *Presidential Courage*. New York: W. W. Norton & Company, 1980.

Murray, Margaret, Theodore N. Pappas, and David B. Powers. "Maxillary Prosthetics, Speech Impairment, and Presidential Politics: How Grover Cleveland Was Able to Speak Normally after His 'Secret' Operation." *Surgery Journal*, Vol. 6 (January 2020): e1–e6.

Murray, Robert K. *The Harding Era: Warren G. Harding and His Administration*. Minneapolis: University of Minnesota Press, 1969.

Nelson, Michael, ed. *Guide to the Presidency and the Executive Branch*, 5th ed. Thousand Oaks, CA: CQ Press, 2013.

Nevins, Allan. *Grover Cleveland: A Study in Courage*. New York: Dodd, Mead & Co., 1934.

*Nevins, Allan, ed. *Letters of Grover Cleveland, 1850–1908*. Boston: Houghton Mifflin Company, 1933.

*Nicholas, James A., Charles L. Burstein, Charles J. Umberger, and Philip D. Wilson. "Management of Adrenocortical Insufficiency During Surgery." *A.M.A. Archives of Surgery*, Vol. 71 (November 1955): 737–42.

Nowak, Martin S. *The White House in Mourning: Deaths and Funerals of Presidents in Office*. Jefferson, NC: McFarland & Company, 2010.

*O'Donnell, Kenneth P. and David F. Powers with Joe McCarthy. *"Johnny, We Hardly Knew Ye": Memories of John Fitzgerald Kennedy*. Boston: Little, Brown, 1972.

*"Official Bulletins of the President's Case." *Boston Medical and Surgical Journal*, Vol. 105 (September 29, 1881): 299–307 and (October 6, 1881): 322–30.

Pafford, John M. *Chester A. Arthur: The Accidental President*. Washington, DC: Regnery History, 2019.

The Papers of Woodrow Wilson Digital Edition. Vols. 62–69. Charlottesville: University of Virginia Press, Rotunda, 2017.

Pappas, Theodore N. "President Warren G. Harding and the 5 Doctors Who Managed His Final Illness." *Annals of Surgery Open* (September 1, 2020): e006.

Park, Bert E. "Woodrow Wilson's Stroke of October 2, 1919." In *The Papers of Woodrow Wilson Digital Edition*. Vol. 63, Appendix II, pp. 639–646. Charlottesville, University of Virginia Press, Rotunda, 2017.

Parmet, Herbert S. *Jack: The Struggles of John F. Kennedy*. New York: Dial Press, 1980.

Pederson, William D., ed. *A Companion to Franklin D. Roosevelt*. Malden, MA: Wiley-Blackwell, 2011.

Pekkanen, John. "The Saving of the President," *Washingtonian*, March 10, 2011.

Petriello, David R. *A Pestilence on Pennsylvania Avenue: The Impact of Disease Upon the American Presidency*. Staunton, VA: American History Press, 2016.

Pinals, Robert S., and Harold Smulyan. "The Death of President Warren G. Harding." *American Journal of the Medical Sciences*, Vol. 348 (September 2014): 232–37.

*Reagan, Maureen. *First Father, First Daughter*. Boston: Little, Brown, 1989.

*Reagan, Nancy, with William Novak. *My Turn: The Memoirs of Nancy Reagan*. New York: Random House, 1989.

*Reagan, Ronald. *An American Life*. New York: Simon & Schuster, 1990.

*———. *The Reagan Diaries, Volume 1, January 1981–October 1985* and *Volume 2, November 1985–January 1989*. Edited by Douglas Brinkley. New York: HarperCollins, 2009.

Reeves, Thomas C. *Gentleman Boss: The Life of Chester Alan Arthur*. New York: Alfred A. Knopf, 1975.

———. *A Question of Character: A Life of John F. Kennedy*. Roseville, CA: Prima Publishing, 1997.

Report of the Proceedings in the Case of the United States vs. Charles J. Guiteau, Tried in the Supreme Court of the District of Columbia, Holding a Criminal Term, and Beginning November 14, 1881. Parts 1, 2, and 3. Washington, DC: Government Printing Office, 1882.

*Reyburn, Robert. *Clinical History of the Case of President James Abram Garfield*. Chicago: Journal of the American Medical Association, 1894.

Russell, Francis. "The Four Mysteries of Warren Harding." *American Heritage*, Vol. 14 (April 1963): 5–9, 81–87.

*Salinger, Pierre. *With Kennedy*. Garden City, NY: Doubleday, 1966.

Schlesinger, Arthur M., Jr. *The Age of Roosevelt: The Crisis of the Old Order, 1919–1933*. Boston: Houghton Mifflin, 1957.

*———. *A Thousand Days: John F. Kennedy in the White House*. Boston: Houghton Mifflin, 1965.

Seale, William. *The President's House: A History*, Vols. 1 and 2, 2nd ed. Baltimore: Johns Hopkins University Press, 2008.

Smith, Gene. *When the Cheering Stopped: The Last Years of Woodrow Wilson*. New York: William Morrow, 1964.

Smith, Hedrick. *The Power Game: How Washington Works*. New York: Random House, 1988.

Smith, Richard Norton. "'The President Is Fine' and Other Historical Lies." *Columbia Journalism Review*, Vol. 40 (September/October 2001): 30–32.

*Sorensen, Ted. *Kennedy*. New York: Harper Perennial Political Classics, 2009.

*Speakes, Larry, with Robert Pack. *Speaking Out: The Reagan Presidency from Inside the White House*. New York: Charles Scribner's Sons, 1988.

Tebbel, John, and Sarah Miles Watts. *The Press and the Presidency: From George Washington to Ronald Reagan*. New York: Oxford University Press, 1985.

*Travell, Janet. *Office Hours: Day and Night: The Autobiography of Janet Travell, M.D.* New York: New American Library, 1968.

*Truman, Harry S. *Memoirs: Volume One, Year of Decision*. Garden City, NY: Doubleday & Company, 1955.

Trunkey, Donald, and Farhood Farjah. "Medical and Surgical Care of Our Four Assassinated Presidents." *Journal of the American College of Surgeons*, Vol. 201 (December 2005): 976–89.

*Tumulty, Joseph P. *Woodrow Wilson as I Know Him*. Garden City, NY: Garden City Publishing, 1927.

Weinstein, Edwin A. *Woodrow Wilson: A Medical and Psychological Biography*. Princeton: Princeton University Press, 1981.

White, William Allen. *Woodrow Wilson: The Man, His Times, and His Task*. Boston: Houghton Mifflin, 1924.

Wilber, Del Quentin. *Rawhide Down: The Near Assassination of Ronald Reagan*. New York: Henry Holt and Co., 2011.

*Wilbur, Ray Lyman. *The Memoirs of Ray Lyman Wilbur, 1875–1949*. Edited by Edgar Eugene Robinson and Paul Carroll Edwards. Stanford: Stanford University Press, 1960.

*———. "President Harding's Last Illness: Official Bulletins of Attending Physicians." *Journal of the American Medical Association*, Vol. 81 (August 18, 1923): 603.

Wills, Garry. *The Kennedy Imprisonment: A Meditation on Power*. Boston: Little, Brown, 1982.

*Wilson, Edith Bolling. *My Memoir*. Indianapolis: Bobbs-Merrill, 1938.

Yale Law School Rule of Law Clinic. *The Twenty-fifth Amendment to the United States Constitution: A Reader's Guide*. New Haven: Yale Law School, 2018.

PRESIDENTIAL LIBRARIES AND MUSEUMS

Grover Cleveland Birthplace Memorial Association: **presidentcleveland.org**
James A. Garfield National Historic Site: **nps.gov/jaga**
Warren G. Harding Presidential Sites: **hardingpresidentialsites.org**
John F. Kennedy Presidential Library and Museum: **jfklibrary.org**
Ronald Reagan Presidential Library and Museum: **reaganlibrary.gov**
Franklin D. Roosevelt Presidential Library and Museum: **fdrlibrary.org**
Woodrow Wilson House: **woodrowwilsonhouse.org**
Woodrow Wilson Presidential Library and Museum: **woodrowwilson.org**

ADDITIONAL ARTICLES FROM THESE SOURCES:

ABC News
Alaska Daily Empire
American Heritage
American Journal of the Medical Sciences
American Review of Reviews
Annals of the American Academy of Political and Social Science
Annals of Surgery
Archives of Surgery
Axios
Baltimore [MD] *Sun*
Boston Globe
CBS News
Chicago Daily Tribune
Columbian [Bloomsburg, PA]
CNN
Daily News [NY]
Daily Public Ledger [Maysville, KY]

Delaware Gazette and State Journal [Wilmington, DE]

Editor & Publisher

Evening Star [Washington, DC]

Fordham Law Review

Fox News

Grand Rapids [MI] *Herald*

Harvard Law Review

Helena [MT] *Weekly Herald*

Indianapolis [IN] *Journal*

Journal of the American College of Surgeons

Journal of the American Medical Association

Journal of the Royal Society of Medicine

Lancet

Missouri Historical Review

Morning News [Savannah, GA]

NBC News

Neurosurgical Focus

New England Journal of Medicine

News [Providence, RI]

Newsweek

New York Herald Tribune

New York Magazine

New York Times

New-York Tribune

NOTUS.org

PBS

Philadelphia [PA] *Press*

Politico

Review of Reviews

Saturday Evening Post

Seattle [WA] *Post-Intelligencer*

Smithsonian Magazine

South Kentuckian [Hopkinsville, KY]

Sun [NY]

Sunday Star [DC]

Telegraph [United Kingdom]

Time magazine

Today's Health

U.S. News and World Report
Variety.com
Wall Street Journal
Washington [DC] *Examiner*
Washington [DC] *Post*
Washington [DC] *Times*
Wheeling [WV] *Register*
Wilmington [DE] *Daily Republican*
X.com

INDEX

Page numbers in **boldface** refer to images and/or captions.

PICTURE CREDITS

Alamy Stock Photo: Associated Press: 211; Zuma Press: 216–217.

Baltimore [MD] *Sun*, November 23, 1963: 169 (bottom left); November 6, 1994: 202 (bottom).

Joseph R. Biden, Jr., letter, July 21, 2024: 224.

Burlington [VT] *Free Press*, November 9, 1960: 160 (bottom).

Chicago Daily Tribune, November 9, 1960: 160 (top).

Chicago Tribune, November 6, 1994: 202 (top).

Daily Public Ledger [Maysville, KY], July 7, 1893: 65 (right); August 30, 1893: 72 (left).

Delaware Gazette and State Journal [Wilmington, DE], August 31, 1893: 72 (bottom).

Evening Press [Binghamton, NY], November 9, 1960: 160 (second from top).

Evening Star [DC], July 2, 1881: 20.

Flickr: FDR Presidential Library & Museum: 124, 126, 129, 134, 136, 137 (bottom), 142, 145 (left); usembassykyiv: 221.

Harper's Weekly, October 1, 1881: 28, 39; June 12, 1886: 56–57.

Helena [MT] *Independent*, July 8, 1893: 65 (left).

White House Photographs, **John F. Kennedy Presidential Library and Museum**, Boston: Abbe Rowe, AR6661-A: 162, AR6646-B: 163; Cecil Stoughton, ST-C277-1-63: 165.

iStock: LennonsGhost: 52; bpperry: 250.

Ithaca [NY] *Journal*, November 22, 1963: 169 (second from top).

Private Collection, **Gail Jarrow**: 102, 119, 122.

Judge **magazine**, September 30, 1882: 41; February 2, 1884: 46; September 27, 1884: 66.

Las Vegas [NV] *Daily Gazette*, September 20, 1881: 30.

Library of Congress, Prints & Photographs Division: LC-USZ62-64278: 12; LC-USZ62-23003: 16; LC-USZ62-77908: 18; LC-USZ62-44266: 22; LC-USZ62-13021: 34; LC-USZ62-98155: 37; LC-USZ62-137259: 48; LC-USZ62-20823: 51; LC-USZ62-48559: 54; LC-USZ62-11984: 68; LC-USZ62-71734: 69; LC-USZ62-105073: 74–75; LC-USZ62-90271: 77; LC-USZ62-13028: 78; LC-USZ62-7633: 81; LC-USZ62-131813: 87; LC-USZ62-62850: 95; LC-USZ62-9980: 97; LC-USZ62-39295: 100; LC-USZ-62-107574: 103; LC-USZ62-65041: 108–109; LC-USZ62-113659: 127; LC-DIG-highsm-47513: 145 (right); LC-USZ62-117124: 148; LC-USZ62-133052: 155; LC-USZ62-13010: 172; LC-U9-1368E-24: 174; LC-DIG-ds-14461: 233 (bottom); LC-DIG-ds-09329: 234; Artist Posters Collection: LC-USZC4-6613: 140; Brady-Handy Collection, 1861-1865, LC-BH826-1483: 26; Cartoon Drawings Collection: LC-USZ62-109585: 86; Genthe Collection LC-G432-0932: 89; Harris & Ewing Collection LC-H27-A-2819: 115; LC-DIG-hec-46907: 132; National Photo Company Collection: LC-DIG-npcc-03619: 96; LC-USZ62-94273: 98; LC-USZ62-32916: 105; Popular Graphic Arts Collection, LC-USZ62-10380: 15; LC-DIG-pga-11215: 233 (top); U.S. News & World Report Magazine Collection, LC-DIG-ppmsca-83290: 159; LC-U9-10623-7: 164.

Life **Magazine**, August 16, 1937: 137 (top).

Los Angeles Times, August 3, 1923: 118 (bottom); November 22, 1963: 169 (bottom right).

Monroe [NC] **Journal**, October 27, 1916: 83.

Politico, July 3, 2024: 219 (bottom).

Puck magazine, May 9, 1883: 43.

The Record [East Bergen County, NJ], November 22, 1963: 169 (top).

The Review of Reviews, August 2, 1892: 62.

Robert Reyburn. *Clinical History of the Case of President James Abram Garfield*. Chicago: Journal of the American Medical Association, 1894: 32.

Shutterstock: ta-24v: 1, 7; Dan Thornberg: 8; Leonorea: 14, 80, 150, 177, 180, 236; Alexkava: 177.

St. Paul [MN] **Daily Globe**, August 17, 1881: 25.

US National Archives and Records Administration: 111-SC-60641: 84; Robert Knudsen, 6816421: 161; Collection RR-WHPO, White House Photographic Collection: 75857029: 180; 75857089: 181; 75857035: 182; 75852767: 186–187; 75852837: 192; 75852869: 194; 6728598: 196; 75854207: 199; General Records of the Department of Housing and Urban Development, 2408428: 203**.**

Wall Street Journal, July 9, 2024: 219 (top); July 22, 2024: 223 (bottom).

Washington [DC] **Post**, August 3, 1923: 118 (top); November 10, 1960: 160 (third from top); March 31, 1981: 190; July 21, 2024: 223 (top).

Wikimedia Commons: 151, 178, 245; Walt Cisco, *Dallas Morning News*: 166; Cecil W. Stoughton: 168; Adam Schultz: 204; U.S. Congress: 207 (top); Office of United States Senator Joe Biden: 207 (bottom); Daniel Schwen: 208; Sgt. Charlotte Carulli: 209 (top); Lance Cpl. Cristian L. Ricardo: 209 (bottom); The White House: 227.

OTHER TITLES IN THE MEDICAL FIASCOES SERIES

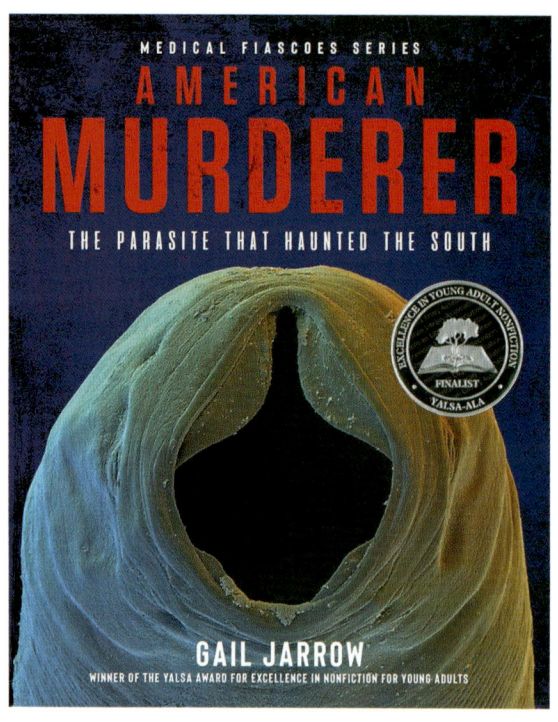

American Murderer: The Parasite that Haunted the South

YALSA Award for Excellence in Nonfiction for Young Adults Finalist

School Library Journal Best Book
(Middle-Grade Nonfiction)

Outstanding Science Trade Book for Students K-12
National Science Teaching Association and Children's Book Council

CCBC Choice
Cooperative Children's Book Center

Best Informational Book for Older Readers
Chicago Public Library

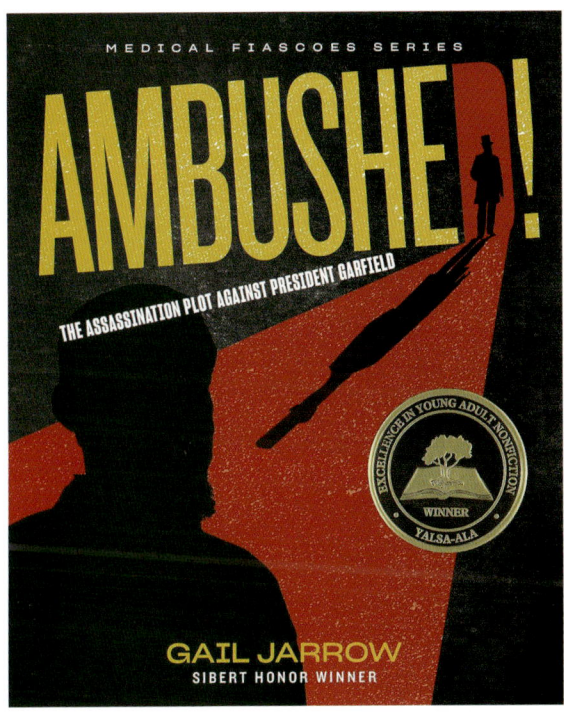

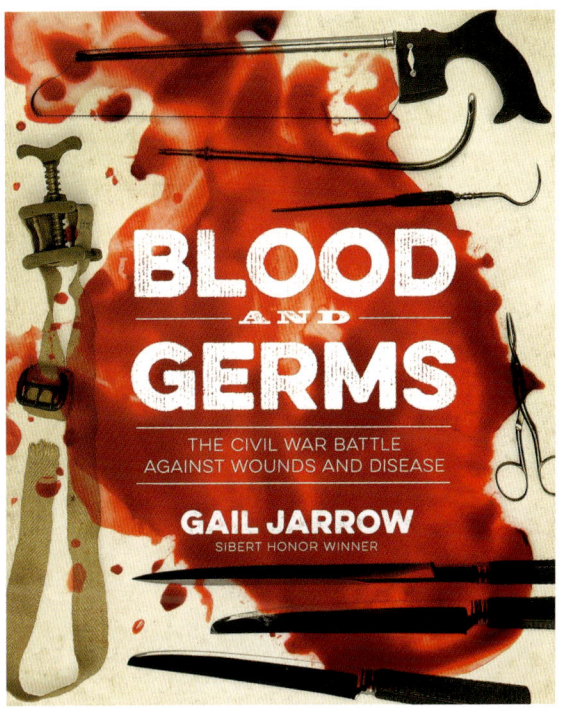

Ambushed!: The Assassination Plot Against President Garfield

Winner of the YALSA Award for Excellence in Nonfiction for Young Adults

Kirkus Reviews Best Book
(Middle-Grade History)

CCBC Choice
Cooperative Children's Book Center

***Booklist**, **Kirkus Reviews**, **School Library Journal**,* Starred reviews

Blood and Germs: The Civil War Battle Against Wounds and Disease

Kirkus Reviews Best Book
(Middle-Grade Nonfiction)

Outstanding Science Trade Book for Students K–12
National Science Teaching Association and Children's Book Council

CCBC Choice
Cooperative Children's Book Center

Orbis Pictus Recommended Book
National Council of Teachers of English

Best Informational Book for Older Readers
Chicago Public Library

GAIL JARROW is the author of nonfiction books about medical fiascoes, deadly diseases, magicians, misinformation, hoaxes, and other fascinating stories from American history. Her work has received many distinctions, including the YALSA Award for Excellence in Nonfiction for Young Adults for *Ambushed!*; the YALSA Excellence in Nonfiction Finalist for *American Murderer*; the Sibert Honor for *Spooked!*; the Charlotte Award for *Blood and Germs*; the Orbis Pictus Honor for *The Poison Eaters*; an NSTA Best STEM Book and Outstanding Science Trade Book; an ILA Best Science Book; and the Children's Book Guild Nonfiction Award. She has a degree in zoology and has taught science to students of all ages. She lives in Ithaca, New York. Visit gailjarrow.com.